Sitting in biology class bored, Jerry grew more and more tired as he waited to go home. He was in his last month of middle school, but he wasn't thinking much about high school. Nothing was particularly special about him. He was pretty average at everything. Most would simply call him a "floater" as he coasted through life. However, by a lottery chance, he was accepted into a prestigious private school 45 minutes away from where he lived. He accepted the offer against his own will. He wanted to roll out of bed every morning and go to his local high school, which was only a couple blocks away. But his parents knew he needed some discipline, so they forced him to go.

As his thumbs mindlessly scrolled on Instagram, he shook. He then couldn't sit still. Central Valley High School's baseball team had just recently been ranked #1 in the county, over three major Catholic schools!

"You good?" a voice came from behind him.

The voice came from one of two very pretty girls in the back. Without thinking, Jerry got up and brought his excitement towards them. Jerry shoved his phone uncomfortably close to their faces.

Toolbox Breakdown on Page 28/29

MISSION STATEMENT

I titled this book "Cancer, I Thank You" with zero intention of being insensitive or downplaying its severity. I understand and sympathize with the impacts this devastation can have on people. That is the reason I am putting my heart and soul into this book. I want to ensure that people who are struggling (not just cancer, but adversity in general) know that they are capable of overcoming any obstacle. I want them to create a life they want to wake up to.

Getting blindsided by cancer myself at just 14 years old, I was exposed to many experiences nobody should have to endure. However, I am grateful. These moments shaped who I am today. Now, I write with the intention of helping *the next kid.*

To that Kid,

I am here for you. I know how it can feel to have the cards stacked against you. I get you. I was there. But I can assure you that you are greater than this. There is nothing your mind can't overcome—including this time.

You deserve happiness. You deserve to feel heard. You deserve it all. That is why I am writing this book for you. I want you to experience what life has to offer. I want you to know there are people who care.

Overcoming this time will transform you into an incredible human being. Then, I ask you to pass it on to *the next kid.*

Love,

Anthony "Jerry" Onnembo

Now let's do this thing together ☺

"That's my school," Jerry said with pride.

"You're going there to play baseball?" one girl asked hesitantly.

"Yes. Yes, I am."

The two girls looked at each other with amazement and they congratulated him. Jerry, standing taller than usual, walked back to his seat. As he sat down, a voice emerged in his head.

Do you seriously think you can play at a school ranked that high? It's even ranked above schools you thought were the best.

There was some truth to that statement. If Jerry wanted to make this happen, his life would have to change. From this point on, Jerry made a commitment to be Central Valley High School's starting varsity catcher as a freshman.

Jerry was no longer just floating through life. He woke up every single day thinking about how he could come closer to this goal. He attacked practices, fighting to become the best he could be.

Nobody had any faith in his goal. His father, Dominick, told him that he thought he should make the freshman team and to "shoot for JV."

His childhood trainer felt the same way. He gently poked Jerry with a bat with each following word:

"You are a freshman."

Jerry didn't say anything.

"How are you even going to do it? It's impossible," the trainer went on.

Although Jerry's mouth didn't make a sound, his eyes did the talking.

"Dominick, this kid is crazy. He really thinks he can do it."

Regardless of their lack of belief, nothing fazed him. He made his commitment and never looked back.

After a couple months, Jerry finally started to be able to hit a baseball with some power behind it. He took pride in that. He genuinely believed that everything was going to be worth it. Not only was he becoming a better player, but also a person. However, the journey was just getting started.

• • •

On a random day in December, Jerry was just cleaning himself in the shower. His body had developed a lot of muscle from his commitment, and he treasured it. But his muscle was more than just that to him. It was a symbol of his hard work. As he applied body wash to his groin, his hand did not go over the surface smoothly. It seemed as if there was a bump. Without much care, Jerry went along with his normal shower. To him, this bump was simply unusual and nothing alarming. However, it was so weird that Jerry decided to show his father.

Jerry walked calmly upstairs. He quietly took his father's hand and put it on his bump.

Having served the country for thirty years, Dominick was a self-sufficient man. Dominick saw the world objectively, a trait that Jerry had always admired. It was incredibly difficult to get to his emotions.

"Ella," Dominick yelled upstairs. "Come take a look at this."

Jerry's mother came hastily down the stairs. She placed her hand on the area with a mother's touch. She did this for a while as she was deep in thought. Her facial expressions told Dominick that something was off.

Although everyone knew something was unusual, Jerry perceived no problem. He thought that Dominick and Ella did not seem worried, rather puzzled.

"Ok thank you for showing us. Go downstairs," Dominick said with a monotone voice.

"Well, what do you think about it?" Jerry questioned.

Dominick took a second.

"You're fine man. Just go downstairs now," Dominick struggled to say.

Jerry listened. If his parents were genuinely concerned, he was unable to tell. Perhaps if he were stronger socially, he could have picked up the subtle clues. But young, naive Jerry went back downstairs to complete his homework.

A little later, Jerry's phone started buzzing. Annoyed with his studies, Jerry instantly grabbed his phone. His eyebrows shot up as he saw DAD across his screen. It was about 9:00 p.m. now. Dominick typically started winding down at this time.

"Come upstairs. We're going to the walk-in clinic," Dominick quickly said.

"What? Dad, do you see the time?" Jerry exclaimed as he sprinted up the stairs.

"We would feel more comfortable," Dominick said while looking at Ella.

Jerry had zero desire to leave the house, but he didn't want to argue. He knew now was not the time to be disobedient. Listening just to listen, Jerry casually put on his shoes.

Dominick and Jerry left without any further words needed.

• • •

All of the local walk-in clinics were closed by this time. They had to drive further to find one that was open. There was nothing stopping Dominick, though. He wanted Jerry to have medical attention as soon as possible.

When they finally arrived, Jerry actually enjoyed the scene. The doctor's office was made to look like a castle. There were many little kids bouncing off of these walls; they loved it! The combination of the laughter and taking a seat surrounded by fake stone walls put Jerry at ease. He even started texting with a classmate about his upcoming test.

Dominick was a whole different story. The lack of seriousness in the environment made his breathing audible. His face blanked like a sheet of paper. His hands twisted into a pretzel. He could only wait to hear Jerry get called in.

After what must have felt like an eternity for Dominick, a voice called for Jerry.

A lady led them into the room. Unknowingly, she was the first medical professional on a very long road ahead.

The room had a childlike theme to it. Inside awaited a cheerful, middle-aged woman. The contrast between her energy and Dominick's was clear as day. As Jerry explained the situation, her positivity grew even further.

"This happens all the time. Don't worry about it," the lady explained with a smile from ear-to-ear. She went on.

"The body has lymph nodes. They naturally expand when fighting off a virus. A virus that you wouldn't even know about! It is really crazy, but I can assure you it's okay."

Dominick was still unsettled. Through a broken voice, he spoke.

"That is great to hear. I'm just shaken by what I saw when I googled."

"Google! Google! Google! Sir, don't ever Google medical information. They will always claim the worst. They would even say this is cancer! There is a 99% chance this isn't that," the doctor exclaimed.

Something changed inside of Jerry. He couldn't believe they were even discussing the word "cancer."

The doctor started again.

"I am not worried at all about your son. Everything is normal here. This situation is a regular occurrence. But, just for our policy we have to send you to a specialist. I know it's very annoying, but I have to follow my rules. You'll be fine though."

Her optimism was hard not to catch. Her positive attitude would have been cherished in any other situation. Here, however, Dominick was still visibly alarmed. As more time passed, Dominick started to feel its effects slightly.

Jerry, on the other hand, stayed relatively even. He gained an understanding of the situation. It clarified his father's peculiar and uncharacteristic actions. Although he learned more about the situation's gravity, it had not yet hit him. His mind was still fogged by studying for his test the next day.

The doctor scheduled an appointment with the specialist for them. Dominick and Jerry thanked the woman for her time, help, and reassurance as they made an exit.

Behind on sleep and carrying baggage (that Jerry had yet to comprehend), Dominick drove through the night. There was no shortage of uneasiness in the air.

• • •

The next day was normal. Jerry, in fact, was loving his life. Although he knew only 3 people going into the whole school of over a thousand, he transitioned into freshman year perfectly. Jerry developed an outgoing, respectful personality that people naturally gravitated towards. His manners made him very popular. He was even starting to develop a relationship with a beautiful girl!

"Ring!" The alarm sounded.

Many people love to hear the dismissal bell go off, including Jerry. But not today. Fun time was over. That sound reminded him about his appointment with the specialist. Even though he wasn't concerned about the medical situation, he didn't like the energy it caused. Jerry's newfound understanding of his parents' behaviors led to a serious atmosphere. He appreciated their care, but didn't want them to stress over him.

Jerry reluctantly put himself on the bus. His parents would be waiting at the stop to head directly to the local hospital.

As Jerry opened the car door, a sense of uneasiness hit him like a charging bull. Before taking a seat, Dominick started.

"Jerry, I got some good news for you. We were fortunate enough to get Doctor Adams today. He's also a surgeon. He's been doing this job for over thirty years. In fact, he's retiring soon and not taking many more patients. I know this is scary, are you okay?"

"Yeah, I'm totally fine," Jerry said honestly.

The rest of the car ride was filled with dialogue between Dominick and Ella. They tried to reassure themselves about the situation. After an extensive discussion, neither one seemed any better.

This talk was just noise to Jerry. His mind was thinking about his life. He took pride in his recent grades, baseball performances, strength, and the new relationships he made at his school. He felt a sense of appreciation that his parents sent him there.

The family pulled into the parking lot of the hospital. Jerry's jaw dropped at the massive size of this place. The parking lot stretched further than he expected. The fact that there were several people making up the valet service stunned Jerry.

Countless employees were standing in the all-white lobby. A solemn sensation filled the air. Jerry realized there was no drawbridge outline surrounding the desk. No screams from children playing tag. No nothing.

Eventually, they made it into their room. Jerry lay down on the bed. As he looked to the ceiling, an overwhelming amount of medical technology hit him. Looking away to his side, he witnessed a massive toxic waste symbol. The room appeared to be closing in on him. The longer he waited, the smaller he became. His parents took notice. Dominick asked Ella for his hoodie and put it behind his head. This simple act pushed the walls further away from him.

"Hanging in there Jerry?" came from a profound voice in the doorway.

"I'm Doctor Adams. It is a pleasure to meet you two," he said while greeting Jerry's parents.

"I read about your report. But, still. Please talk to me about everything."

Dominick gave him an elaborate breakdown. Every minor detail under the sun, Dominick had it covered.

After a long talk, Doctor Adams examined the area. Within a minute or so, he asked to perform an ultrasound.

"Is that a needle?" Jerry questioned. "I hate needles."

"No," Doctor Adams said laughingly.

Jerry then witnessed the first sign of humanity.

"You know Jerry, I still don't like needles. I know I operate on people for a living, but it doesn't bother me. However, when I receive them, different story. I get the same feelings as you."

"See Jerry," Dominick interjected. "He's a surgeon and doesn't like them."

This light-hearted conversation occurred as Doctor Adams pulled an ultrasound out of the thin air. A feeling of trust arose in Jerry. As soon as this sensation came, the room fell silent as Doctor Adams applied the machine to the lump in Jerry's groin.

A couple minutes later, the judge had come to a verdict.

"We're going to need to perform a biopsy on it. We cannot confirm whether it is cancerous or not. In order to be safe, we want to physically test it. However, I am 90% confident it is not cancerous. Everything will be okay," Doctor Adams said in a monotone voice.

Jerry's mouth made a wide circle. Oddly enough, the concept of surgery didn't move him at all. He understood that doctors put patients under anesthesia and he wouldn't feel any needles. What threw him off was the fact that Doctor Adams mentioned a number. Something seemed suspicious to Jerry about these numbers. Knowing he wouldn't be able to figure it out, he let it go.

Doctor Adams then scheduled an appointment to perform the surgery. The family thanked him for his time and care as they made an exit.

Unsurprisingly, the car ride home was similar to the one there. Jerry was still relatively unfazed. His parents' dialogue was continuous; all one big noise maker to him. However, the air became even heavier.

About a week later was the same car ride back to the same place. Feelings of hunger dominated his senses as he couldn't eat all day. However, he even prepared for the fasting. The day prior he stayed up eating heavily until 11:50. After consuming an unhealthy amount of food at one time, Jerry worked out incredibly hard. He wanted to compensate for the time that would have to be wasted. Time that can't be put into baseball.

Jerry comfortably lay in the bed. The objects that made his hair stick up just a week prior no longer bothered him. The thought about anesthesia eased his mind. However, this imagination quickly came to an end as Doctor Adams entered the room with a nurse.

Doctor Adams was wearing a Superman logo on his scrubs, not very fitting in relation to the surroundings. He explained that since Jerry was a big guy, the anesthesia needed to go through an IV. The nurse had a portable table, tubes on it, and a smile on her face.

"You'll be okay," she said with a hint of cheer.

The nurse handed Dominick an icepack as they approached the bed.

Dominick came alongside Jerry. He held the icepack on the back of his neck with one hand, and stuck out two fingers with his other. He told Jerry to squeeze these fingers with his right arm. The intention was to help him relax his left arm so they could get the IV in. However, Jerry squeezed those fingers with his whole body.

He tensed.

“Do you want to get stuck more than once?” said the nurse.

To Jerry, that comment was so stupid that it didn’t warrant a response—only a thought in his head:

Does she really think I want another one?

At the time, Jerry couldn't comprehend her rhetorical question. His mind was flooded with negative emotions.

“Then you have to relax,” exclaimed the nurse.

Those comments did nothing as he flexed intensely. She understood the situation and tried another approach.

“Do you play any sports?”

“I play baseball,” Jerry mumbled.

“What position are you?”

As Jerry went to answer, the needle punctured his skin. Her plan worked to perfection. Instead of telling him to relax, she took it upon herself to naturally relax him.

The IV was successfully in. Before he got into the operating room, they wanted to draw some blood. Since the IV was already in, Jerry didn't even think twice. However, as the blood was sucked out of his body, he turned green.

The nurse got the blood. Jerry got a nickname.

"He's the hulk," Doctor Adams said to Jerry's parents.

Unknowingly to him, that name stuck and even became useful. Dominick would tell the "Hulk" story to warn future nurses when they attempt to stick Jerry with a needle.

Jerry's parents both reached over the bed's plastic arms and gave him a kiss. Jerry felt sensations of sorrow as the nurse wheeled him away from them. At this point, he couldn't wait to go unconscious.

Wheeled into the operating room, they laid him down on this massive platform. Doctor Adams introduced Jerry to the people above him, but eventually it was too overwhelming. There were several people each performing a job on something.

Strapping him down, adjusting his blood pressure cuff, aligning his body, everyone seemed to be doing something.

There then came a point where everything shifted. Only one distinct event occurred. A woman placed her head over his face and asked him a very familiar question.

"What sports do you play?"

"I play baseball," Jerry said as he moved his eye to the upper left corner.

There were two women. One was working on something, while the other was monitoring his vital signs.

"What position do you play?" asked the woman with her face uncomfortably close to Jerry.

Before Jerry had the chance to answer, his consciousness slipped away. The next thing he knew, he was in the post-operating room looking at his father.

"Where am I?" Jerry asked.

Dominick rushed over.

"Jerry. Are you okay? We are here for you. Do you need anything?" Dominick asked immediately.

"Yeah, I am okay. I just really want to leave. I'm sweating really bad," Jerry said.

He was right. Sweat ran down his entire body.

Dominick immediately went to the nurse stationed outside. She claimed there was not much she could do.

A minute later she came into the room with a glass of cold water and apologized she couldn't do more. Jerry thanked her for the water and she left.

"The surgery was a success. Doctor Adams said if this is cancerous, he might have got it all out. Meaning that, treatment may be unnecessary. But he said he thinks there is a 50% chance it is not cancer."

"Dad. It's over. I got it," Jerry said.

"Stop that Jerry. Don't say that. That is not what the doctor said," Dominick snapped.

Jerry looked at his father very intensely and somewhat annoyed.

"Dad. Think logically. Are you kidding me? We went from 99% to 90% to 50%. Do you not see the trend? I got it," said Jerry with a weird uncertainty in his voice.

Dominick hesitated.

"Well, I would like to hear from the doctor," Dominick said softly.

For the past couple of days, Jerry could still only hobble. His walk was so awkward that teachers let him leave class early. However his mind was fine. He was just annoyed that he couldn't use his time better. Then, he created a way. By putting his left leg behind his right, he believed there was no strain on his groin while doing push-ups. Once Jerry found this out, he abused it. He remembered sweat falling from his face at 1 in the morning.

Jerry had found his outlet—and a problem one night.

"Mom. Dad," Jerry yelled in the morning. "Come take a look at this."

They never like hearing those words come out of his mouth. But they ran to Jerry immediately. He showed them his groin.

The incision site was inflated like a water balloon. It was obvious liquid had accumulated under the skin. Interestingly, there was a hint of yellow to this water balloon.

Dominick called Doctor Adams immediately. He managed to get an appointment the same day, only in a couple of hours. Jerry couldn't wait to go see him.

After another desolate car ride, they made it back in the same spot—the very room where Jerry became "The Hulk." He really started to miss the fake stone towers and pictures of alligators. But he took some deep breaths and pretended he wasn't there. Luckily, the wait wasn't very long.

"Hello again everybody," Doctor Adams said with a slight smile. "Your surgery went very well initially. I believe I removed the entirety of the tumor. But what do we have here?"

"His incision is protruding and the whole area around it is liquid. It's even yellow. Do you really think this was a successful surgery?" Dominick responded with worry.

"I definitely do. This inflation is just a normal complication. Nobody can control it, but it's an easy fix. I just have to drain it. You'll be out of here very soon," Doctor Adams casually said.

"Drain it?" Jerry gulped. "What do you mean?"

"Oh no, Jerry it's nothing. I have to suck the fluid out or it can get infected. You won't feel a thing because I cut your nerves. You won't even know it's happening," Doctor Adams said confidently.

Although his statement sounded logical, it was useless. Jerry jumped at the sight of a big syringe.

"Jerry, come on. Relax. The longer you do this, the longer we stay here. Don't waste this man's time," Dominick lectured.

Jerry sighed.

"Give me your hand," Jerry asked as he understood his father was right.

Squeezing his father's hand, he shut his eyes. Jerry's mind went blank, but was working at a mile a minute.

A couple seconds later he heard a voice.

"All done. I told you that you wouldn't even know," said Doctor Adams jokingly.

"No way it's done," Jerry exclaimed with a smile.

"I told you it'd be easy. Come on, you have to admit that wasn't so bad," Doctor Adams said with a chuckle.

Jerry was really fond of his lighthearted tone. Conversations like these are what made Jerry trust him.

“Oh it was terrible. So incredibly painful Doc,” said Jerry as happy as ever.

“Can’t even give me that kid. Tough cookie you guys have here,” Doctor Adams said as he looked at Jerry’s parents.

“Whatever Jerry,” He went on.

“This fluid is usually fine, but we have to check it because of policy.”

Dominick’s guard shot up. It was noticeable.

“What!” Dominick blurted out in an instant. Panic was in his voice. “We have heard that policy thing before. We don’t like it.”

Before Dominick could get another word in, Doctor Adams cut him off.

“Relax,” he said with a genuine tone and face.

Doctor Adams became a regular person, connecting with everyone on a deeper level.

“Everything is fine,” he repeated towards Dominick and Ella numerous times.

He turned to Jerry with a smile.

"You have one thing to do. Go enjoy Christmas. You deserve it."

• • •

A couple days had passed and Jerry finally regained his body's strength. He attacked the opportunity to exercise and play baseball. These outlets had totally taken his mind off his groin. He felt like just a normal kid again.

Out of nowhere, Jerry's parents called him upstairs unexpectedly. With tears blanketing their eyes, his parents were unusually close to each other on the couch. Their serious tone instantly changed his carefree mood. Taking a seat, he grew increasingly uncomfortable as his father tried to mutter out words no 14-year-old expects to hear: He had been diagnosed with a rare type of lymphoma. His jaw hit the floor as his ordinary life had just turned upside down.

After a brief discussion, Jerry quickly ran back to the basement. Instead of his usual activity, he ran into the laundry room. Sitting on the floor, back against the dryer, Jerry folded into his knees with a river coming down his cheeks.

The gravity had finally hit him.

With tears covering his face, Jerry mustered up the courage to stand up. He went into the bathroom. A split-second decision with lasting impact on his life arose. As he stared at himself inches from the mirror, he knew his life wouldn't be sustainable in self-grief.

Is this how we're going to go out? Jerry asked as he stared down the man looking back at him.

The voice went on.

You have worked too hard on yourself. You must become the starting varsity catcher. This can't be the way everything ends.

Jerry thought about these words. The voice was true.

Suddenly, a tiny spark of hope arose within. Wiping some tears from his eyes, he completely engulfed himself in this sensation. Unbeknownst to him, this seemingly small ember morphed into something massive: the necessary key he needed to maintain his "word," or promise to himself. Playing varsity baseball became more than just a goal, rather a challenge to his character.

This vivid flame threw him onto the floor, forcing him to do countless monotonous push-ups. Repetition after repetition, he strangely enjoyed watching pools of sweat accumulate on the floor. His arms quivered as his nose repeatedly touched the puddles beneath him. With his upper body barely capable of simple movement, he stood up. Although he had lost all feeling in his arms, he regained it in his mind. He confidently walked back to the bathroom mirror, but something was different. "He" was no longer. The same kid drowning in self-grief just minutes prior had vanished into the abyss.

Grief and cancer had suddenly lost its grip. The negativity mindlessly thrown at him from his family and closest trainer disappeared. Only faith survived. Faith appeared to revive that big-hearted child and his imagination. With nobody in his corner, he had himself. Looking at his reflection, he profoundly smirked, yearning for the challenge.

• • •

March. Walking into school the day of the tryouts, Jerry felt something special. He threw his massive equipment bag over his shoulder, like a Navy SEAL ready for combat. Although baseball is just a sport, he wasn't there to "play." He was there to conquer any obstacle in front of him. He had a greater mission: keep his "word" to himself, as he was all that he had at this time. He was the freshman that showed up every day 45 minutes before school to sharpen his dull skills. Hands layered in blisters, body shaking to fight off hypothermia, or sleep deprived, nothing mattered—he still showed up to that desolate batting cage. Even though these moments quickly became dark and lonely, they were necessary. They were stepping stones to his pursuit of fulfillment.

As he stepped onto the field, he unwaveringly stared at two other seniors that were also competing for the honor of being the starting varsity catcher. He eyed them down, way past the point of awkwardness.

There was no doubt or worry in his body. All of the work behind-the-scenes started to reveal itself. And eventually, he did it. Jerry earned the position of Starting Varsity Catcher. Batting third and catching every game, Jerry was a main contributor to the team as a freshman. More importantly, he had turned into the person his younger self crying in the mirror dreamed about.

Very few people truly understood what this accomplishment meant to him. He always kept his problems and desires to himself. However, he whole-heartedly appreciated the process, especially the devastation. Through reflection, every experience that cancer threw at him became a lesson. Therefore, without the cancer, Jerry wouldn't be the person he is today.

Those lessons are too powerful to just stay with him.

They must be given to "the next kid."

So here we go

Suffering only remains suffering when someone doesn't learn from it. Once somebody can take away meaning from their terrible experiences, those experiences are no longer terrible. They are useful for goals and betterment of oneself.

Understanding this concept, Jerry dug deep in his experiences trying to extract a larger purpose. He found and kept what was useful. He threw away what wasn't.

He separated his "toolbox" into three categories focused on different things:

Seeing — how he viewed reality to keep his inner peace

Giving — how he cultivated beauty for others

Making — how he built the life he refused to let cancer take

Each category propelled Jerry towards his goals, but more importantly, they improved his character and quality of life.

Here it is:

Measuring Tools

Gardening Tools

Power Tools

"Come on Jerry, let's go. Get upstairs, you know we have an appointment to meet the doctor today," Dominick cried downstairs. "Don't make us late, man."

Jerry came upstairs fairly quickly.

"What are you talking about 'meet the doctor'? We've been to Doctor Adams a million times!" Jerry energetically said.

"No, no, no. We were assigned to a new doctor. We have to go to New York City," Dominick casually responded.

"What! Why?" Jerry snapped. "But I loved Doctor Adams."

"It's out of my hands. We have to go to her," said Dominick.

"Answer my question. Why Dad?" Jerry demanded.

Dominick took a breath.

"I didn't want to tell you this. I was hoping you wouldn't care," Dominick said while he looked down at the carpet.

"The type of lymphoma that you have is extremely rare. It's actually so rare that our hospital transferred everything to a lady named Doctor Trella. Turns out, they even misdiagnosed you!"

Dominick moved closer.

"Jerry, I love you. I want what is best for you. These doctors are literally ranked the best in the entire world. People come from all over the planet to go here. No exaggeration. They have your back."

Jerry's hair stood straight up.

"What do you mean it's extremely rare?" Jerry gulped.

"Stop! Don't be scared. The survival rate is incredibly high. Thank God. However, only about 100 children in the world get it a year," Dominick instantly threw at him.

Dominick gave Jerry a bear hug and whispered in his ear.

"I am comfortable that you will be okay. I have your back. Trust me." A couple hours later they arrived.

"Hello gentlemen. My name is Doctor Trella. It is a pleasure to meet you," said an elderly woman in a charming voice.

Everyone discussed the situation and Jerry came to some realizations. It appeared to him that Doctor Trella's mouth couldn't keep up with her mind. She might be the smartest person Jerry had ever met. Hearing her explain the diagnosis sounded like gibberish to him. However, this gibberish allowed Jerry to take a breath.

Not only was Doctor Trella a genius, she was also an angel. Being from an underdeveloped country, she had to earn her Ph.D. from Notre Dame. In her spare time, she founded a cancer hospital for children in her homeland.

"See why we have to be here Jerry," Dominick said with a smirk.

Doctor Trella chimed in.

"Jerry, can I tell you something?"

Jerry immediately shook his head yes. To him, she had instantly reached Aaron Judge status.

"You may know that the radiologists at your previous hospital misdiagnosed you. It's actually kind of funny. Those radiologists actually used to be students of ours," Doctor Trella said proudly.

Dominick broke out laughing.

"That is crazy. There is no way that doesn't make you feel safe," he said while looking at Jerry.

"However," Doctor Trella started again. "We can't really even shame them. Your condition is incredibly rare. We have seen a couple cases like yours though."

“Wow. Okay then,” Jerry said in a shocked voice. He continued.

"I have a question for you Doctor. Do you know what caused it?”

“Unfortunately, we do not. Our hospital is always doing research though,” Doctor Trella replied.

“But he is a young guy in very amazing shape,” Dominick butted in.

“Doesn’t matter,” Doctor Trella said. “There was nothing you could have done to prevent it.”

Those words echoed in Jerry’s head.

There was nothing you could have done to prevent it. There was nothing you could have done to prevent it. There was nothing you could have done to prevent it.

• • •

The statement from Doctor Trella had been ingrained into Jerry. It didn’t sit easy. He wrestled with the fact that he was powerless.

Jerry wanted to be able to have some control over his body. After staring mindlessly at his pop-up table that served him as a desk, he thought of a question. Jerry hoped this question could bring him some security.

"Hey Dad," Jerry screamed while running upstairs.

"What in life is guaranteed?" Jerry asked. He was desperate for an answer to fill this hole inside him.

Dominick smiled.

"Well son. There's a famous expression by Benjamin Franklin. 'The only thing guaranteed in life is taxes and death.' But hypothetically, you don't have to pay your taxes, you would just be in big trouble."

"Are you kidding me? The only thing guaranteed in life is death. That's the saddest thing ever," Jerry replied and shook his head. "Isn't that just lovely?"

"I can guarantee you a hug right now," Dominick said with a smile.

Jerry gave him a hug and went back downstairs. He had so many thoughts just rushing through his mind. He even started talking to himself.

By this time, he could see the darkness fall as he looked up in his basement window. That's when Jerry thought something weird.

I am going to sleep soon. It's not even guaranteed that I will wake up in the morning.

Jerry's goosebumps had burst out of his skin. He was now terrified and ran to his mirror. Searching for a way to change this, he realized he couldn't.

Subconsciously, Jerry had let out a sarcastic smile of defeat. He held it for a second. That fake smile had slowly turned real. He realized that it was all he could do. He finally found something he had control over.

Jerry had slept like a baby that night.

Tool Acquired: Presence

APPLYING THE TOOL

Jerry understood his health wasn't guaranteed. But he found a smile that was.

Find yours.

"Ding. Ding," The elevator sounded as Jerry and his parents got off at floor 9, the pediatric level.

As soon as the elevator door moved itself out of the way, a collage of exciting colors engulfed the wall in front of him. Although Jerry initially smiled, his bright expression faded. He stopped for a second and looked closer.

Color Therapy was written on a piece of paper. Jerry shrugged in confusion. He didn't get much time to think it over as a massive cart filled with desserts followed behind him.

They approached the front desk.

"What's your birthday?" the lady at the desk asked.

Unbeknownst to Jerry, every adult would ask him that simple question everywhere he went.

"March 10, 2008," Jerry responded like a zombie.

The lady put a white band around his wrist.

"You guys can have a seat right over there," the lady said as she pointed to a beautiful waiting room.

Jerry tried to follow her finger, but his vision was blocked by a vibrant fish tank. Then, it hit him.

The room had come straight out of a movie. There was a new color in every direction Jerry looked. Between the artwork, sculptures, LED lights implanted into the walls, funky furniture, this was the coolest place Jerry had ever been in.

Except one thing.

Although the designs of the chairs were extremely bright, the room was dark. Numerous exhausted families were there. Many looked like they were going camping. Amidst each family, was a child with a white band around his wrist.

As Jerry took a seat, he tried to make zero eye contact. He didn't want to make anyone feel even more uncomfortable. However, he did notice something strange.

Taking a deeper look at the artwork, Jerry realized it was too imperfect. Sloppy handwriting blanketed pieces of neon-colored construction paper. There was no way that the best hospital in the world wanted to display this artwork.

The art looks like it was made by little kids, Jerry thought to himself. *Could this be related to color therapy?*

Jerry had made himself incredibly curious. He had to look around the room a little more.

Straightening his back, he made quick observations of the room. He noticed that many white-banded kids were remarkably young. Jerry prayed they didn't understand the gravity of the situation.

One table stuck out amongst the others. A mother and a father sat across two dressed-up adults, one with a lab coat. The mother held a hairless child on her lap. The father tried to throw words towards the lady with a lab coat, however nothing happened. There was an invisible wall between them.

The man sitting next to the lady with the lab coat tried the same thing—but with a different result. This man's neck would turn to the opposite party every five seconds. He created a bridge between the infant and healthcare.

Suddenly, their child sprinted past Jerry. He had a green dinosaur bandage wrapped around his arm. Sticking out of the bandage was a tube with a green cap. Regardless, he was sprinting head-on to the gigantic wall made of glass.

Jerry clenched up. The stillness in the room tied him to his orange seat. His lips were sealed to shut to speak.

The toddler had surprisingly stopped. His hand reached for a doorknob bigger than him. He had just shown Jerry a new universe.

For a split second, the thick air had been interrupted by an upbeat, child-like song. These sounds sparked something in Jerry.

Now Jerry was unwaveringly staring at this abstract glass wall. Through certain pieces, he caught enough glimpses to understand what was occurring.

Multiple adults with hats and glasses were jumping around. A massive table filled with food was surrounded by many bright plastic balls. Dancing underneath the vast array of decorations, toddlers partied like it was 1999.

Their beautiful hearts had been condensed and protected in this magical room.

Dominick had poked Jerry in the shoulder.

"Yo buddy come with me. I have a question for the front desk," Dominick said in a regular tone.

The two of them were waiting in line for the front desk when a haunting voice spoke in a secluded room behind him.

Jerry turned.

"Kids walk very fast in the hallways. Backpacks are very heavy. The medicine we're giving you will make school too hard. We don't believe you can go," a woman said softly to a little child sitting alone.

Jerry froze immediately.

Why was the kid all alone?

Five seconds later, he ran to the bathroom lined with vibrant tiles. Jerry put his hands on the sink and his mind replayed an old scene he didn't even know he had.

• • •

Jerry was in the fourth grade. He was in the bathroom at a Halloween Trunk-or-Treat just washing his hands. Without a problem in the world, Jerry looked to his right to see his friend, Marcus.

Marcus was wearing an all-black robe that was held tightly by a belt. LED lights outlined his costume. Marcus's hood was up exposing his whole face. With reading glasses and a mole on his cheek, Jerry noticed something.

"Is there candy in your mouth?" Jerry asked jokingly.

"Ewww!"

They both smiled wide at each other and Marcus's blue lips were as clear as day.

"Your lips are blue!" Jerry energetically said as they walked out of the bathroom together.

Fast forward a year, Marcus had been diagnosed with cancer and was forced to miss a whole year of school. Marcus went from a key part of Jerry's friend group to barely heard from.

• • •

Jerry looked up at the mirror. Then he looked to his right and saw Marcus's blue lips.

The color therapy had just clicked.

"Bang. Bang."

The beautiful depiction of fish on the door seemed to jump.

"Jerry! Let's go, they are calling for you," A strong voice came from behind the door.

Jerry's parents were accompanied by a young female nurse.

"Nice to meet you, Jerry. My name is Kiara," she said in a cheerful manner. "When you're ready, we're ready."

"Let's go I guess," Jerry responded.

The group of them headed to the back towards the chemotherapy chambers.

Passing the party room on his left and the waiting room on his right, Jerry came to a fork in the road. He could understand how people would fall into the waiting room. However, he embraced the path that the color therapy revealed.

"What is your birthday?" the young nurse asked. Jerry looked down at his white-banded wrist and smiled.

"March 10, 2008 was the day I was born," he said with excitement.

An hour later Jerry was all set up. Attached to a clear bag with a toxic symbol on it, two IVs were in his arm. Although it was only 9 a.m. in the morning, the doctors told Jerry's parents they would arrive back home the next day.

"Jerry!" said a young blonde woman walking in the prison cell. "How are you doing bud?"

"Doing great," Jerry responded quickly. "How are you?"

The woman's eyebrows went to her hairline.

"I love this energy! But this isn't about me. It's about you. Jerry, if you could have one wish in the world, what would it be?" she eagerly said.

"I don't know," Jerry responded.

"I would like to know this as well," Dominick chimed in.

Jerry smiled and made eye contact with the lady.

"I wish to know why you are asking," Jerry said with a laugh.

"Good lord. I like you kid," she chuckled. "I am with the Make-A-Wish Foundation and we would like to offer you any experience you want. You can go anywhere or meet anyone. Your wish is our command. What would you like?"

Jerry fell silent as images circled through his head.

"I would like you to save your money. Give it to one of those kids in the waiting room. I don't need it."

Tool Acquired: Perspective

APPLYING THE TOOL

The “waiting room” is dangerous, but unfortunately, it is very easy to slip into.

Although the party room is super close to the waiting room, they are miles apart.

Jerry was offered anything in the world from his chemotherapy chair. But he couldn’t ignore that pair of blue lips to his right.

The chair stayed the same. Jerry didn’t.

Look to your right.

"Hey bud, I got you this," Dominick said as he handed Jerry a red plastic cup.

"You got me a cup of ice?" Jerry questioned. "Where did you even get this?"

Dominick pointed to a wall directly across from them. In between the LED lights implanted on the wall, he could see an opening.

Jerry blankly stared. He was confused that there was a doorway with no door.

"It's just a pantry Jerry. You can get whatever you want. You just have to watch what you can eat sometimes when you are in here. You have to today," Dominick said.

"What do you mean I have to watch what I eat?" Jerry inquisitively asked.

Jerry followed that up immediately.

"Are you calling me fat?" Jerry said with a smile.

Dominick started.

"Jerry, you notice how we didn't give you breakfast today. Ella and I also took away the snacks by your bed. That wasn't an accident. You need to get a CAT and a PET scan today. You aren't allowed to touch food until after."

Dominick took a breath.

"But let's go check out what's in there for after you are done."

Jerry agreed and they walked towards this mysterious opening.

As they turned the corner they were met with an abrupt stop. Jerry felt a sense of claustrophobia coming from a spacious walkway. Surrounding them tightly were walls of cabinets.

Doing a further investigation, he realized that all the shelf space was covered with an item. However, the selection was scarce. The whole menu was either saltine crackers or a small cup of cereal.

He turned to his right to see a refrigerator taller than him. He grabbed the steel handle and pulled.

Met with numerous cartons of milk, Jerry was unfazed. As he looked at the many rows of milk lining the shelves, several plastic containers caught his eye.

He picked one up.

"Dad, look at this sorry sandwich. It's just cheese and bread," Jerry said laughingly "It's actually pathetic at this point."

"Put that down," Dominick replied in an annoyed tone. "Let's get out of here."

"Yeah okay, you're right. I'll put this depressing thing down. I think I'd rather eat Mom's disgusting mac and cheese," Jerry chuckled with a wide smile.

Throughout the next five hours, Jerry had been put in multiple foreign machines, all cold and plastic. Being forced to hold many positions like a statue, Jerry felt a void deepening in his stomach.

Jerry's hands were tied above his head as a young man put his face uncomfortably close to his.

"I am going to put a fluid through your IV. It will feel like you are peeing. Trust me - I've been doing this for five years, you won't actually be peeing," he said with charisma.

Jerry never felt comfortable moving his arm with an IV in it. Throughout every experience, his elbow would always be at a 90-degree angle pinned under his chest.

As the man reached for his IV, Jerry squirmed.

"Just work with me," he said.

The nurse helped Jerry slowly extend his arm until the wire could reach a tiny box on wheels.

Instantly, cold sensations shot right through the empty gap in his stomach towards his groin. Jerry really believed he was peeing.

Jerry also smelled this strange liquid. After a minute, he realized it was coming from his breath. This sensation had reached all parts of him.

Jerry's body went back and forth through this machine. He looked up and saw three faces attached to the plastic above him. One had a wide smile, one was neutral, and one had a deep frown.

The face with the deep frown was blinking.

The family had finished the intensive scanning and returned to the ninth floor. Due to Jerry being a minor, he must go to the pediatric level to get his IVs removed every time.

"Ella," Jerry cried desperately as they sat in the waiting room.

Jerry looked like a beaten-down car. His heart was emotionally empty, while his stomach was physically empty. The difficulty of the day had made him sit still, practically unresponsive.

"Yes?" Ella normally responded.

Jerry had mustered up the strength to turn and look at her.

"Do you have any food in your pocketbook? My stomach is eating itself," he said before he returned to his blank existence.

"No, I don't. I'm sorry," Ella said as Dominick chimed in right after.

"After we get the IV out of you, let's stop in the pantry."

Unwaveringly watching the door of the IV room, Jerry waited for a nurse with a clipboard to peek their head out. Eventually, it was his time. He had never been so happy to hear his name be called in that room.

When they took off the bandage surrounding Jerry's IV, they also ripped up his arm hair. Typically, Jerry would bounce like he was at a trampoline park. However, he stayed still. His mind was stuck on the prize: the pantry.

Jerry sprinted out of the room with his dad trailing behind him. He turned the corner to the same place he found himself before. However, something was different.

"Don't get the cereal. We're going to the car now. I don't want it to spill," Dominick said.

Jerry couldn't care less about that statement. He wanted it. And he wanted it now. If Dominick wanted to stop him, he would have to be prepared for a fistfight.

Jerry opened one of the vast arrays of cabinets. His findings had matched his stomach—empty.

Desperate at this point, Jerry threw open the refrigerator door. The absence of the milk cartons made room for only one item: a cheese and bread sandwich.

The sandwich was sitting on a throne made of gold. This massive display of beauty in a plastic container had stayed there the whole time. It had been waiting for Jerry to come back.

Jerry immediately snatched this sandwich. He held the cheese and bread triangles to his chest like it was his baby. Nobody would have been able to take it from him.

As Jerry's teeth sunk into food, his eyes and head slowly turned up. The simple combination of cheese and bread had made sense. Every bite was just right.

“Nothing has ever tasted so good!” Jerry said happily aloud as he devoured the magnificent treat.

• • •

Jerry had always played a lot of sports growing up. Though he was average at everything besides baseball, his parents forced him to play high school soccer. Since soccer was a fall sport, they had practices starting in the summer. Having these practices gave him the opportunity to know a couple faces in the sea of over a thousand strangers on the first day of school.

Jerry knew the first day of school wouldn’t be easy, but he felt it was necessary to transition into his new school. Turns out, he was right. The first day of school was incredibly hard.

On the morning of the first day, everyone was thinking what outfit they should wear or what hair style they should do. They felt the magic of the day.

On the morning of the first day, Jerry was thinking why they needed two IVs of chemicals going into his arm. He felt the heaviness in the room.

Jerry's eyes widened when they couldn't reschedule his chemotherapy date. Dominick assured him that he tried, but the hospital was too structured and busy.

Jerry's face was slumped down for hours. He believed it would be harder to work his way in the school now.

"Dad, are you kidding me? I can't believe I am actually stuck here. Probably until tomorrow like the last time!" Jerry exclaimed. However, he tried to stay calm. He did not want to move his robotic arm.

"I know you are upset, but we have to do this. Your health always beats everything. There is nothing Ella and I would put above it," Dominick replied.

Jerry felt the truth of his words. He was right.

"Excuse me," Jerry said to a nurse. "Do you think I can go to school tomorrow? Today was my first day."

"Jerry, I am sorry to hear that. That really sucks," she paused. "You can go if you feel okay."

"Bang," Jerry whispered.

He knew where he would be tomorrow morning.

• • •

"Ring! Ring! Ring!" the alarm clock sounded.

As Jerry went to turn it off, he realized it had the number "8" on it. It was 8 a.m. He was late!

"Mom! Mom! We are late to school. We got to go. Who would set the alarm to 8?" Jerry yelled as he rushed to find his clothes.

"I did," Ella said. "Your father and I decided we wanted to let you sleep to recover from yesterday. We already called in late. Everything is fine. We'll leave in 15 minutes. You'll be there for 8:45."

"Are you sure?" Jerry questioned with uncertainty.

In the back of his mind, he agreed with their decision. He really appreciated the extra sleep. In no healthy way would Jerry be able to get back home at 1 a.m., have that medicine in him, and catch the 6:45 school bus. He understood there was no more getting up at 7:30 and rolling out of bed to his local middle school, but his body needed the rest.

"More than sure," Ella responded with a smile.

She was right. Jerry had arrived in the middle of his first period—history. The class was at the opposite side of the school.

Jerry entered the school, feeling lighter than he had in a while. His body moved freely through the thin air. Dopamine rushed through him as he felt at ease. The ordinary lockers, the classrooms full of strong kids, the teacher's voice yelling at them—it was heaven.

Although these classrooms were not as colorful as the waiting room, they were brighter.

As Jerry turned the corner, he approached a long hallway. All the way at the other end were two boys Jerry had met at soccer practice. They weren't really even his friends; they were acquaintances at best, but nothing stopped his mouth.

"Yo! Yo! Yo! What's up guys? How we doing?" Jerry screamed across the hallway as a large smile grew on his face.

The physical distance separating them had made this encounter awkward for the two boys. However, Jerry couldn't care less.

They smirked at each other. Jerry's energy was contagious. In an upbeat tone, one started.

"Why is he so happy?" he loudly said, looking at Jerry.

"Bro, you know summer just ended right? How are you this happy?" the other immediately followed up.

"Just happy to see you guys," Jerry responded with his same energy.

"They don't know," Jerry said under his breath as he turned into class.

Jerry took a seat in the front row. He placed his bag next to his desk and felt the chair before sitting.

Cold and plastic.

Jerry's body sat down, but his spirits went up. He loved the vertical position that his uncomfortable chair put him in.

Jerry had never paid so much attention in class.

Tool Acquired: Gratitude

APPLYING THE TOOL

The Cheese and Bread Sandwich is always just a sandwich.

You decide how it tastes.

About halfway through the first month of school, Jerry successfully made the transition into the new environment. He had developed many relationships with everyone: teachers, students, principals, and even janitors. Jerry just tried to be his high-energy self and people naturally gravitated towards that.

This seamless transition made Jerry's confidence go through the roof. He even started to do things that were totally foreign to him just months prior.

"Can I have your number?" Jerry asked the blonde girl sitting next to him in class one day.

Her name was Lily. She was in almost all of Jerry's afternoon classes, including chemistry. Her charismatic personality was what compelled Jerry to ask for her number. She always wore the biggest smile…or at least he thought.

It was a normal day. Jerry was just casually walking down the hallway towards his chemistry class when he heard screams.

The peaceful nature of the scene had vanished. Forceful soundwaves bounced off hundreds of ordinary lockers. These screams were propelled further by the light air.

From out of nowhere, a girl sprinted past Jerry with her face in her hands. He turned and blocked traffic immediately. He took a second in an attempt to recognize that person.

"That was Maya," Jerry mumbled.

Maya was a quiet girl that was best friends with Lily. He sat next to her in Italian class. She didn't want to talk to anybody, including the teacher. However, she was still always nice to everyone she came in contact with.

Jerry picked up his pace to reach his class. Bursting through the door, he couldn't wait to speak with Lily.

As soon as the teacher stopped talking and allowed the class to get to work, Jerry shot right over toward Lily's desk.

"Hey Lily, I just saw Maya running down the hallway crying. I think you should go check on her," A crushing weight evaporated off Jerry's shoulders.

"Yeah, she's alright. Thanks for asking," Lily replied.

A small smirk grew on Jerry's face. In his playful tone, he spoke.

"She probably got a 98, instead of a 100 on her Italian test."

Steam rushed out of Lily's nose as her face became red. She snapped.

"Don't say that. You don't know what other people are going through," Lily scolded as she walked away. Her footsteps were audible.

Jerry's ankle started to bounce.

Those words penetrated right into Jerry. They were sharper than any pain he'd felt being in the hospital 14 hours yesterday while receiving chemotherapy.

Instantly, Jerry had words spiraling up his throat. Thankfully, his mind stopped

everything. He must not let his emotions give away his medical secret.

Zero thoughts ran through Jerry's mind as he stared at the cabinets ahead of him. In his peripheral vision, he watched Lily laughing as she joined another chemistry group.

After a couple empty minutes, Jerry found it within himself to stand up and do the same. He thought it was actually better to not work with Lily anymore. He was too smart for her…or at least he thought.

Once Jerry got home, "you don't know what others are going through" ran through his head like a hamster on a wheel.

"How do you say something like that and not apply it to everyone. She didn't even live by the words she had just spoken. How ironic," Jerry looked up, shaking his head with a sarcastic laugh.

But why? Why couldn't she see it? She's smart, Jerry thought to himself extensively.

Flashbacks of the two boys in the hallway on the first day of school started to play in his head.

"Why is he so happy?"

"Bro, you know summer just ended right? How are you this happy?"

Lily's statement went through Jerry's head again.

They weren't right. They assumed. Jerry said in a soft tone.

The statement went through Jerry's mind for the last time; however, this time he was looking at the person's eyes in the mirror.

You don't know what others are going through.

Jerry's jaw dropped in a combination of shame and embarrassment. His quick-wit was becoming more toxic than the chemotherapy.

Figuratively and literally, Jerry knew the feeling. He couldn't give to others what the doctors were pumping into him.

• • •

Ella never appreciated how the school bus would always arrive at school at 7:20 when school started at 8:00. Her enthusiasm for this topic was overboard, but Jerry could understand some of the frustration.

Jerry didn't complain every second like she did, though. He just enjoyed the time as he walked around the hallways with his friends. Their little "walk and talks" always lightened Jerry up and set the mood for the day. Not today, though.

Something was off from last night. After he tossed and turned all night, something had to change. Jerry wasn't sure how, but he'd find something.

The school structure was similar to a square. As he walked down the hallway, Jerry searched for any opportunity. He was ready to move mountains.

Jerry walked past the cafeteria as he turned a corner.

There were two doorways into this vast space. Jerry froze in one and observed.

Everybody ahead was giggling as they bounced off the walls. The spirits of this room had reached above the ceiling.

Except for a dot in his peripheral.

There was a boy sitting on the floor with his legs outstretched out in front of him. His computer was plugged into the wall as it was low on energy. However, the energy should have gone to a much more needed place—his heart.

Crowds of people were standing over this boy. They were greeting each other and holding full conversations over him like he was invisible.

Although the boy was only a couple inches from these people, they were miles apart.

Jerry knew what had to be done as he pushed through the swarm of people.

"How you doing brother?" Jerry said as he extended his hand. "Take my hand, will ya?"

The boy's eyes shined bright as he immediately grabbed his hand.

"I'm Jerry, nice to meet you. What's your name?"

"I'm Raul. Nice to meet you too," the boy said in a surprisingly friendly tone.

"I got some people for you to meet," Jerry said with heightened cheek bones as he introduced him to his friends.

The new and improved group had walked some laps around the school. Turns out, Raul was from the town next to them. Jerry used this common ground as the basis of the conversation.

Raul's computer was completely dead in comparison to his energy. Not a moment went by without someone in the group laughing. It felt like the bus had arrived at school at 7:59.

Not only was the morning brighter, Jerry was able to take a breath. This was exactly what he needed.

Tool Acquired: Empathy

APPLYING THE TOOL

Lacking empathy is a cancer. Thankfully and ironically, Lily was able to call Jerry out.

From understanding the situation, Jerry turned those words on himself.

It was there that he found real chemotherapy—not the same kind your classmate in chemistry class might have got for 14 hours yesterday.

Don't scold your lab partner.

"Hey Jerry," Ella called downstairs. "Do you want to come with me? I am going to pick up food from Grandma's. You should get fresh air."

Jerry was relaxing downstairs on the couch in recovery from one of his surgeries.

"Are you kidding me Mom?" Jerry replied with a hint of anger. "Don't tease me. I could barely walk."

"I think this could be good for you. You haven't left the house in a couple of days," replied Ella.

Jerry lost some control. The house felt it.

"What do you want me to do? Want me to go run a marathon? I didn't choose this."

The following silence was loud.

Dominick felt his bedroom walls rumble and charged out.

"What's going on down here?" Dominick questioned as he hustled down the steps.

"Mom is pushing my buttons," Jerry responded. "She basically called me a cellar dweller. She acts like I want to be stuck here."

"Ella definitely has got her moments. But how did this start?" Dominick asked calmly.

"She asked me if I wanted to go see Grandma," Jerry said with a little shame.

Ella crept her way downstairs.

"Well, why don't you? It could give you someone different to talk to. I personally think you should," Dominick said while looking at Ella in agreement.

It had become a two against one, but Jerry was ready. The day before he had seen an Instagram post. In the picture it said:

WORRYING DOES NOT SOLVE TOMORROW'S PROBLEMS. IT JUST TAKES AWAY TODAY'S PEACE.[1]

He had so much time to reflect on this simple line. He thought deeper about this concept than anything else in his life.

"Why would I do that," Jerry strongly fought back. "What does she know about cancer? What can she bring to the table? You need to go to Harvard just to be able to slow down those doctors."

"Come on Jerry. It's not about that. She can make you feel better," Ella replied.

Jerry responded immediately. He knew his position was fool-proof.

"I would feel fine if you guys could see the bigger picture. Answer me this question: would Grandma worry about me if we told her the situation?"

"Of course she would," both of them responded instantly.

"How would that help me?"

The crickets started chirping.

"It would only hurt her. You better not tell Grandma."

Jerry replayed countless scenes of him and Grandma. They made pizza together, he jumped on her trampoline as she watched outside with joy, and the numerous times they collected figs from the trees together. It was too precious. Grandma was incredibly deserving of the homerun ball that Jerry had run off the field to give her after he hit it.

"I love her too much," Jerry yelled. "Don't you dare tell her a thing."

"But she is your grandma," Dominick said, confused with his son.

"I never said she wasn't," Jerry said.

Dominick was not giving in.

"She has the right to know."

Jerry shook his head immediately. He took a deep breath and continued.

"No. She has the right to peace."

What in the world, Dominick thought to himself as he sat quietly looking at Ella.

"Dad, look. Worrying will not fix anything. I will still have cancer. All worrying will do is hurt my grandmother. I can't live with myself knowing I dropped that bomb on my grandmother."

"It's not a bomb. It's just your situation. Don't call it that," Dominick rebutted.

"Sure. You can call it that," Jerry stated. "But it would be coming across in a sympathy-inducing way. I am not a victim. I refuse to be. I am just like everyone else."

Dominick's teeth were starting to show as his cheekbones raised. He looked at Ella who wore a frozen expression and then turned to Jerry.

"You know what son. I respect you a ton for that. You are way tougher than I ever was at 14."

Jerry instantly chimed back in.

"This statement is not about being tough. I just love my grandma and want to do what is best for her."

"You're a tough little cookie," Ella said anyway.

"No I'm not. Stop saying that. I just understand that the more you think of something, the more power you give it over you. I promised myself I will give cancer nothing."

Dominick looked down as thoughts flowed inside of him.

Did I teach him this and don't remember. How could he say he is trying to protect grown adults from a disease he has when he is 14. This kid is a lunatic. How in the world?

He sifted through all these ideas until he found something he could say.

"Well Jerry this is hard for someo…"

"It is only hard if you think it is hard," Jerry yelled before he could finish his breath. "Now knock it off."

Dominick waited a second and tried again.

"Well, you can always come and talk to us. We can help you get through this."

"Dad, I thank you very much. I love you for that. But I will never accept it. If you help me get through it, then I won't become as strong as I could have when I get through it. Besides, the time will eventually pass."

Dominick looked at Ella. They shook their heads in disbelief.

"You know you can always come to us if you need it though," Ella threw in.

"Yes. I am aware. Thank you for that," Jerry said.

Dominick and Ella looked at each other. Then at the same time they spoke.

"We won't tell Grandma."

• • •

When Doctor Trella heard Jerry didn't want to tell anybody, nothing happened.

"Everybody handles things differently," she told Dominick and Ella. "Just by law, there are a couple people that have to know in the school. One administrator, the nurse, and his athletic coaches."

When this information was relayed to Jerry, his face turned red. However, his parents explained that they wouldn't say a thing.

"But they are human. They're going to gossip and everyone will know," Jerry yelled.

"You don't get it Jerry. This is professional. They could be in serious legal trouble if it gets out. They can't and won't say a word. Trust me. I'm under similar rules in my job." Dominick explained and went on.

"You don't even have to tell them. The hospital will send out formal emails. Trust me. You're good."

"Alright. If this information gets spilled, I am out for blood," Jerry said without a laugh in sight.

"Ring. Ring. Ring," a wired phone mounted to a wall sounded during class.

The teacher picked it up and faced the class.

"Jerry. They want to see you in guidance," the teacher said.

Without a word, Jerry lifted himself up and walked to guidance. He had never actually been there. Besides a couple brief emails, Mrs. Fitzgerald—his guidance counselor—was a complete stranger.

He found a room labeled Mrs. Fitzgerald and hoped for the best.

"May I come in?" Jerry asked politely as he held his hand on the doorknob.

"Please do."

Jerry pulled this little piece of metal towards him and stepped into this new atmosphere.

"I'm Mrs. Fitzgerald. It is truly a pleasure to finally meet you. I have heard so many great things about you," she said as Jerry looked around this tight enclosure.

"It is nice to meet you too," Jerry said as he outstretched his right hand towards her.

"I can't wait to be a part of your future success here," she exclaimed as Jerry pulled his chair out.

Jerry had let out a wide smile, part due to being uncomfortable.

"Thank you," Jerry sounded through the large gap in his front teeth.

"Well, Jerry," she started.

"I just wanted to call you down to ask if you were okay."

"Why wouldn't I be?" Jerry asked.

"Well, being your guidance counselor, I have to hear some things. But you can trust me though. I will never say a word to anybody about anything," Mrs. Fitzgerald said in a genuine tone.

"I'm okay, thanks for asking," Jerry quickly responded.

"Jerry, I just want to make you aware of a service we have here. We have an absolutely fantastic wellness center just down the hall." She pointed in the direction, but Jerry refused to look.

Instead, he stared her right in the eyes as a smirk grew on his face. No words said.

Mrs. Fitzgerald threw her hands up like she was getting arrested. She shook her head as it went in a downward motion.

After a moment, she dropped the act and her polished white teeth shined bright.

"There are a lot of people that go there for way less things," she said.

"I'm sure they do," Jerry responded.

He felt like he had won the lottery. The legs on his chair were off the ground. Like Aladdin on his rug, Jerry used the chair to fly away.

Thank you Cancer, Jerry mumbled under his breath.

Tool Acquired: Peace

1-Quotation by Randy Armstrong

APPLYING THE TOOL

Worrying gives external things power over you. It is a thief of your energy.

Jerry had cancer. His grandmother didn't need to.

She didn't have the right to know. She had the right to peace.

Protect your grandma.

Note: If you are struggling, please reach out to a medical professional or trusted adult. Protecting peace is not the same as suffering silently.

One day, Jerry and his family sat in the waiting room just looking across the pathway. He stared at the party room in an attempt to feel how the toddlers did. However, through the thick fog of sadness, it was hard to catch more than a glimpse.

"I told you my Giants would stomp on your little team," yelled a young girl's voice. It seemed to have been coming from the IV room. It continued.

"It's okay. You have next year," she said with a boatload of sarcasm. "I hope our success hurts."

A faint voice tried to argue back. Jerry was barely able to understand it.

"Did you not see the referees? They let you guys win. They feel sorry for you."

The girl had just come out of the room. Standing in the hallway, she poked her head in.

"Keep crying," she chuckled.

The girl moved her dinosaur-bandaged arm to her face. The green-capped tube nearly hit her as she moved her wrists underneath her eye like a baby bawling.

Jerry's eyes widened as he loved what he saw.

This girl was probably about Jerry's age. Her head shined, but her personality really shined. Her social skills blew Jerry's out of the water. She lit up every tile that was under her.

Although she was now walking forward, her presence stayed behind.

Until she froze.

She stayed intensely still and tilted her head to the side.

"Oh, no. Sarah, what could you possibly want from my life?" exclaimed a male nurse at the other side of the walkway. "I'm innocent."

She moved as he approached her.

"I know. I know," she replied. "But you're still very handsome."

"Get out of here Sarah. I'm married. I love my wife."

Sarah looked to her side and started over.

"What an unlucky woman she is!" Sarah gave him a side eye. "Did she willingly marry you?"

She stretched that "you" out with sass.

"Get outta here," said the man as he gently nudged her away.

"Ok, have a great day Nick!" Sarah yelled as she started skipping down the hallways.

She had made it about fifteen feet and froze again. This time there was nobody to be seen—or so Jerry thought.

Sitting in the corner of the waiting room was a young Jewish couple. The woman held the baby as tears came down her face. As they stood up walking over to the nurse that had just called them, the man placed his hand on his woman's back. They slumped with their heads down, taking their time with each step.

Sarah had a target.

In a blink of an eye, she teleported there and spoke at the speed of an auctioneer.

"Hi guys. My name is Sarah. I just want to let you know that you will be okay. They are super nice in there. You have nothing to be scared about."

The couple barely even turned their heads as they were fixated on their child. However, she walked alongside them and continued.

"If you need anything just let me know. Again, my name is Sarah and I am here for you guys," with a smile as wide as her face.

The couple stopped for a split second and both turned their heads. They thanked her and both groups went their separate ways.

But, this time, the couple's backs were a little more straightened.

Sarah had walked past Jerry with her chin up and chest out. Her steps moved the thickness of the air aside, making a way for her to go.

I want to marry something like that.

He daydreamed about a wife like that raising his future children.

"Jerry," a short blonde nurse called, snapping him out of his head.

"Let's go," Dominick said.

The group followed the nurse into the IV room.

"I'm Jessica. Nice to meet you guys."

"Nice to meet you too," replied Jerry.

Standing in the doorway, Jerry still felt what Sarah had left behind.

Jerry continued following her and found a tiny room, divided into three stations.

Beside each divider was a nurse with a package of tubing and green caps, not a sight Jerry did cartwheels over.

Alongside his mother were cabinets that looked way too familiar.

"Are there sandwiches in here?" Jerry questioned the nurse.

"No, silly. Look at that over there," replied the nurse as she pointed to a poster.

Prize Menu, Jerry read aloud.

"Why is there the word 'menu' with toys? Can I eat the toys?" Jerry's thoughts were audible.

The nurse explained how it was a sign to show all the little kids. When the kids are done, they can choose something. The nurses sometimes got lucky and it relaxed them, as they were fixated on the prize after.

"It's not going to fixate me. I know you have a needle," Jerry nervously laughed.

"He's going to make you earn your money today," Dominick chimed in to the nurse. "One doctor called him the 'hulk' because he is big and turns green."

"Alright, so this is what we are working with here. I got it. We've done this many times before," Jessica responded. "We'll be fine."

"You need me?" A set of eyes popped around the divider.

"I was just going to ask for you," Jessica smiled and continued as Jerry sat down.

"Trust me we are going to be okay Jerry. Well, except for this one thing."

Jerry gulped as Jessica stared him in the eye. Her hands were on her hips.

"We ran out of green dinosaur bandages," she turned and then held out her hands. "Would you rather princesses or ponies?"

Jerry broke out laughing as he reached for his father to lean on. Time had suddenly stopped.

• • •

"Achoo! Achooo!" Dominick sneezed as he sat with Jerry in a medieval castle.

Horses representing all different colors were racing back and forth through the dirt pit in front of them.

"Let's go blue!" 10-year-old Jerry screamed at the top of his lungs.

There was a man on top of each horse. Each man was holding a very long stick that Jerry, at the time, thought was a baseball bat.

The blue was sitting in the far corner of the arena. He was kicking his feet back like he was digging a hole.

Directly across from them there was a horse wearing a red bag. The horse's eyes were the same color as blood. The man on top of the horse held an evil smirk.

"Boooooo," Jerry yelled as the announcer focused on them.

Many people agreed with Jerry. A wall-shaking roar burst out for the blue horse, while nothing was left for the darkness on the opposite side.

"LET THE FIGHTING COMMENCE" an announcer yelled.

The two horses had left their corners in a hurry. They were going to ram into each other head-on.

At the very last second possible, the blue horse shifted to its side—too fast for the red horse to comprehend.

The blue man with the baseball bat had poked the villain. The red horse was left all by itself.

Alongside everyone in their section, Dominick and Jerry sprang out of their seats. The sporting event had become louder than a concert.

"BLEED BLUE, BLEED BLUE, BLEED BLUE" erupted from the masses of people surrounding Jerry.

Without thought, Jerry had fallen into this spirit. With every inch of his lungs devoted to this sound, he grabbed his father's hand. Eventually, he sat down and took the deepest breath of his life.

• • •

"I'll take a blue pony," Jerry said like a child.

"They don't actually have ponies here, you big dummy. It's only a bandage," Dominick laughed and looked at Ella. "I mean you can't make this up."

"Actually, we do!" Jessica shrieked and looked at the Prize Menu.

She stepped out of the room.

Jerry looked at the other nurse. She simply shrugged her shoulders.

Moments later Jessica arrived back with a step stool.

"Watch this," she said.

Jessica put the step stool on the ground and stretched her whole body to the top cabinet. She was just able to access the cabinet's mysteries.

Stepping down, Jessica covered her hands. She walked to the table as she put her hands behind her back.

"I'll make you a deal," she said with a grin as she uncovered a blue pony figurine. "If you make this easy, Bluey is all yours."

Jessica placed Bluey in the back of the table, as if he had his own corner to defend.

"Ok ok. Let's get this over with. Give me the largest knife you got," Jerry exclaimed as he stuck out his forearm.

As the two nurses approached him, Jerry's body became a cylinder block. His hands bounced quickly as his muscles acted like he was doing a bench press.

"You need to relax," said the other nurse in a childlike tone. "Jessica won't let you have Bluey if you don't."

Jerry immediately pictured his basement. He was lounging on his gaming chair as his friend's voice came through his headphones. His feet were elevated on his desk.

He took a breath and all the stress held in his frame had vanished.

The nurses pounced on this opportunity like a lion hunting for food.

Ten seconds later, a clear tube connected to his arm fell off the table.

The one nurse picked it up and ran cold saline water through it. Jerry felt the sensations flow through his arm.

"All done," Jessica excitedly announced. "See, that wasn't so bad."

"It wasn't the worst thing in the world," Jerry grinned. "My mom's mac and cheese is way worse."

Everyone broke out into laughter, including Ella.

Jerry put pressure into the floor as he tried to elevate his body. His head felt like a pillow. Stars emerged in his vision as he sat back down.

"You alright Jerry," Dominick instantly asked.

Both of the nurses were ready to act.

Jessica reached for an ice pack. She put it behind his neck.

"Dominick," called Jessica. "Hold this ice pack for him please."

Dominick went for the ice pack. Jessica went for the magic.

"You really earned this," Jessica said as she grabbed Bluey and handed it to Jerry.

Instantly, Jerry's mind wandered.

BLEED BLUE. BLEED BLUE. BLEED BLUE.

His ten-year-old self had run in his veins and into the plastic tube. His spirits had escaped, way past the limitations of the green cap.

Jerry stood up.

Although he took two steps forward, his presence was left behind.

“Ahhhhh. Ahhhhh,” came from a voice at the station farthest from him.

The screeching voice was from a little girl. Her little body was bouncing off the walls. Her parents were crowding around her, just trying to at least keep her in a seat.

Ella and Dominick had walked out of the doorframe, but Jerry froze.

He had a target.

Although he didn’t have Sarah’s conversation skills, Jerry knew what had to be done. He must give it everything he had.

“Excuse me,” Jerry said in a shy voice.

The little girl had stopped for a second with a curious face.

“Here take this,” Jerry stretched out his arm with the blue horse in it.

He turned to the parents.

“Everything will be okay. Trust me.”

“Thank you!” the little girl said with genuine happiness.

"My pleasure," Jerry said as he skipped out of the room.

Tool Acquired: Empowerment

APPLYING THE TOOL

Sarah didn't know Jerry was watching. Jerry never spoke one word to this amazing girl. You don't know who is watching you right now.

Bluey was just a plastic horse. But thanks to Sarah, Jerry made it more.

Act like Sarah.

"Honk! Honk!" sounded a little red horn from across the waiting room.

Jerry turned in his seat as he was facing the fish tank, however his mind was stuck on the fish. He wondered how they could have so much energy.

"Don't they get tired just swimming in circles?" Jerry asked his parents who were alongside him.

"You see this one Jerry," Dominick said while pointing at a catfish. "It looks like he is kissing you, but he's not. He's cleaning the tank. That's why they're so common in big fish tanks."

"Honk! Honk!" sounded again.

Since Dominick was going to continue on about catfish, Jerry became overly fascinated with the scene in front of him.

There was an adult with a red button nose, a horn in his hand, and a red wig. He galloped around the swarm of little kids around his feet. His polka-dotted outfit read *Dancing Red Clown.*

The other adults were wearing white coats with pens in their front pockets. Each one of them had a necklace with a picture of their face on the front.

"Ayyyy," exclaimed an adult throwing his stethoscope around like a lasso in a squatting position.

Although he was full of energy, his other hand had a clear container with leaves in it. A spoon rested on top of it in a cubbyhole. He pushed his black boots into the ground in an attempt to raise himself.

The Dancing Red Clown dashed over and put his mouth to the man's ear, totally breaking a happy character. With a sense of worry through the white makeup, they spoke.

The man looked at his colleagues and shrugged. He then disappeared into the backroom.

The Dancing Red Clown had started to twist and turn all over the floor. The kids shrieked as he went past them doing an amazing worm.

How could this all be happening in my waiting room. This isn't a club.

All the kids then chased the clown all over the waiting room. Eventually, he succumbed to the normal customs of the public and played dead. The children took this opportunity to use him as a trampoline.

“If only someone can help me?” the clown cried very loudly.

Suddenly, a big clown wearing black boots appeared from around the corner and screamed.

“I can!”

The adults in white coats started dying of laughter. Their faces turned purple as they gasped for oxygen. They each put down their clear containers and picked up their phones.

As the black-shoed clown approached the gang of kids, he became unsure of what to do. He lowered his body onto his knees and outstretched his arms.

The Dancing Red Clown immediately sounded.

“What are you doing? There are no hugs in war!”

Before the man could even process, a child was charging him like a bull. The child put his head into his chest. The fake clown’s back banged against the ground behind him.

“Down goes the clown. Down goes the clown,” the children chanted.

A roar erupted amongst the man’s coworkers. They each grabbed onto the person nearby to stop themselves from falling.

"Let's go!!!!" the Dancing Red Clown screamed as he gave the child a high-five.

The fake clown lay on the ground like he was an outline at a crime scene. His mouth grew a smirk.

After a minute, everyone helped pull the man up.

Some dark curly hair from the floor didn't match the red wig. The Dancing Clown helped the man reorganize himself.

A woman from the group spoke.

"I got the whole thing recorded. You are never going to live it down."

"I'm sure. I'm sure," the man replied, shaking his head and smirking.

"Well," another woman spoke. "Let's get out of here while we still have some time in our break."

The man took a step back and looked at all the kids. Regardless of the bandages holding tubes on their arm, they smiled as they stared back at him.

With their smiles rubbing off on him, he spoke.

"Nah, you guys can go. I guess I'm working overtime today."

The group turned around and abandoned their friend.

"He's going to be starving," one woman said to another.

"No he won't," she responded. "He'll be full."

• • •

On a random winter day, Jerry was walking the streets looking for houses to shovel. He chose to take on jobs alone—he hated splitting money. Jerry wanted every dollar for himself, regardless if it meant more work.

By the time Jerry was walking, most of the houses were already done. He had walked so far and had no success. His shoulders started to slump.

He turned around and just went home.

As he was walking home, he noticed an elderly woman looking out her window. She was staring at her car with a sense of worry.

The car lay in a field of white powder. With the powder on every inch of her property, there was nothing she could do.

Jerry took this opportunity as he ran up her snow-covered stairs and rang her broken bell.

"Hello. Can I shovel you out?" Jerry asked her.

She was a fragile old lady. Her white hair barely reached past her shoulders. She spoke in a soft voice.

"Sure, but I will pay you for it."

"Yeah, that's what I was asking. What do you think is fair?" Jerry responded politely.

"Can you do thirty?" she replied.

Jerry turned and looked at her vast property. The plow trucks created a mountain at the end of her driveway.

Walking to her stairs, he remembered his foot didn't go all the way to the ground. It felt as if he was standing on a taller floor.

"I'm sorry. This is a lot. I think 50 is fair," Jerry honestly said.

The woman unhappily agreed and Jerry put his head down and started.

He tried to throw his shovel in the rock-solid snow. With each attempt, the shovel recoiled as it was too puny for the task.

50 wasn't enough, he thought as he wrestled with the mountain.

"Excuse me," the lady called from her window. "How did you know I needed help?"

Jerry smiled without even thinking.

"I was just walking around looking for houses to shovel. I saw you haven't been shoveled out yet."

"Well, thank you so much!" she responded with a cute tone.

Jerry felt that she was the grandma who would take care of a stranger with soup and cookies. His hands worked twice as fast.

After his shovel was screaming for help, Jerry had eventually made some progress. The mountain blocking the apron had rolled away. The true black color of the driveway revealed itself.

The elderly woman rushed out of her house as quickly as she could.

"Thank you so much for this! I was really worried about my car's engine. I am going to take it around the block to just get it moving," her face shined bright.

"Can you make a little pathway to my garage, too please?" She said with puppy dog eyes.

"Of course. I got you," Jerry responded as thoughts flew through his head.

This isn't what we agreed on. This is messed up. But how could you argue with her? She's such a little cutie.

The lady started the car as Jerry reluctantly walked towards the garage.

When he opened her fence, Jerry realized the job would be nothing—especially compared to what he just did.

Within a matter of a couple minutes, Jerry had totally moved every speck of snow on her beautiful walkway. The path consisted of tiles that were a work of art.

Instantly, Jerry was taken back to his grandma's house. His grandma had a pathway that stretched out the size of her yard. That trail consisted of very similarly sculpted tiles. There was a small outline between each tile. Jerry deeply bonded with his grandmother while prying out the weeds in the gaps with a fork.

The elderly lady had returned with cheer on her face. She had walked towards Jerry.

"It is amazing! I love it," She went past Jerry and dug into her garage. "I'll pay you in a second. Let me just put some salt on the amazing work you did."

Jerry followed her and outstretched his hand. He wanted the word "pay" to come sooner.

"Let me help you," he said.

"Why, thank you! You're the sweetest!" she replied as she reached for another cup.

When she made the reach, her body started to tilt sideways. She attempted to grab onto a nearby cabinet.

Without any hesitation, Jerry threw out his wingspan. He covered the lady's waist with a bear hug and squeezed. He stayed still for a moment and no words came out of his mouth.

The lady was able to stay vertical due to Jerry's solid base.

"You saved me! You're the best! Thank you," the woman screamed.

Jerry wrapped his arm under her armpit.

"Don't thank me. Let's just get you inside. I'll salt the pathways so that doesn't happen again," Jerry calmly said as he walked her into her house.

He dropped her off at the door and retrieved his shovel. He widened the pathways even more before he dropped a ton of rock salt on the ground.

The black tar stuck out as if it was the middle of summer.

Jerry approached the door.

"I believe my job is done. I did the best I could for you," he smiled.

"Oh please, you're fantastic. Come on in. You're not a stranger. I'm Mila. Pleasure to meet you."

Jerry took a step in as he was hit with a strong wind of smoke. He went no further than the welcome mat.

The darkness of the room made an uncomfortable sound: silence.

"Before I pay you, are you hungry? Thirsty? Anything?" she pleaded.

"I'm all good, thank you though," Jerry replied calmly.

"Where are you from?" she questioned in a friendly tone.

"I live just a couple blocks away. I'm very close to middle school and high school," Jerry responded. He started to become more comfortable in this woman's house.

"Wait. What's your father's name?"

"My dad's name is Dominick," Jerry grinned.

"Dominick! I love Dominick. You look just like him," Mila said as her face lit up. "He is a wonderful man. No wonder why he has such a gentleman as a son."

"Thank you," Jerry chuckled. He felt something brewing inside of him. "How do you know him?"

"Well son, being in the town as long as we have, I have gotten to be quite friendly with him. He's easy to get along with though," Mila said as her face refused to dim. She continued.

"We could go on all day, but I am sure you are tired. I don't want to keep you for too long. I owe you 50."

She reached for a thin envelope and pulled out several pieces of paper. They all had the number 1 in the corner, except one.

"Take this," she said while she handed Jerry $20. "I owe you thirty more."

She looked around and started to whisper as she moved closer to Jerry's ear.

"I can't give you these singles. They are for my cigarettes."

"That's okay. I understand," Jerry said in a normal tone.

"I am sorry that I am whispering. My son lives in North Carolina and has cameras above us. I don't want him to know how much I smoke."

Jerry couldn't help but giggle. Mila then continued in a normal tone.

"The bank is closed right now, but you can stop by here on Monday to pick up the other 30. Well, you can stop by whenever you want—the door is always open for you."

"Here, take my phone number," Mila said as she reached for her flip phone. "Please remind me to go to the bank, though."

Something didn't feel right to Jerry. His stomach felt empty; Jerry even heard it growl like he hadn't eaten anything all day. He took a second.

The man with the dirty red wig popped into his head.

I guess I'm working overtime today.

With a smile he spoke.

"You know what, forget about the 30. I'm good," Jerry exclaimed. He then paused for a moment.

"I will take your number though. Let me know if you need help. I got you," he said while he took a picture of Mila's flip phone number she had written down on a sticky note.

"What? Are you sure you don't want anything?" Mila said on the brink of tears.

Jerry responded with a huge smile.

"I want you to stay warm. It's cold out there."

Tool Acquired: Service

APPLYING THE TOOL

Money is super cool. It can do a lot of things.

However, it can never fill the "hunger."

That void is way deeper than anything money can buy. Only service can fill.

Jerry gave back the $30. Give back yours.

"You alright there Jerry?" Dominick asked as they drove to the hospital.

"Yeah, I'm fine. Why wouldn't I be?" Jerry asked with a hint of confusion.

"I mean you are getting surgery today. I've seen you hide under tables when you get a flu shot," Dominick said as Ella chimed in.

"You look more comfortable right now than when I wake you up in the morning. Something is going on."

Jerry's eyes wandered off into the glistening Hudson River. One ear was blasting rap music while the other heard his parents' concerns.

"I'm going to get knocked out," Jerry calmly said.

"What?" both of his parents screamed.

"Who are you fighting?" Dominick immediately followed up.

"Not like that, you two dummies. I mean I am going to go under anesthesia. I won't even know needles are going into me. I'll be on another planet."

"Yeah, that's right," Dominick grinned. "How did you know that though?"

"I did my research," Jerry responded. "If I didn't know that I'd be flipping out right now. It's funny how you guys knew that too."

As Jerry got out of the car beside the hospital, he looked up. Row after row, it just kept towering. The building appeared as if it was directly above him. Jerry recalled memories of him playing with building blocks when he was just a toddler.

Although the building seemed to rise, he didn't.

The family stepped in and had reached the elevator. Dominick's finger didn't reach as low on the keypad as it usually did.

You are going to get knocked out. Jerry reminded himself as he gulped. He took in the scene in front of him.

The strange number 3 was blinking.

The familiar number 9 was just in the background.

"*Ding!*" The massive steel door had moved to the side, revealing new scenery.

Jerry was met with faded white walls, boring wood planks, and a massive plant with only a couple of leaves.

"How could something be so big and afraid to grow more leaves?" Jerry said as he pointed at the plant like it was just an object. Dominick and Jerry both chuckled over the unfunny joke.

Going further in, the family took a seat in the desolate waiting room. Each seat was spaced apart, with nothing but air above them.

There were also tiny wooden walls that separated sections of the room. Jerry wondered how someone could see the few magazines if they were boxed in.

Jerry felt easy as the room did not radiate white light off the walls. However, his chair was not pink. It was just a chair.

"Ay Dad," Jerry said in a soft voice looking at Ella. "This room is as bland as mom's mac and cheese."

The three of their faces lit up—the only thing in the room with true color.

"Jerry," called a woman.

Jerry rose and walked through the jungle of nothing. His family trailed.

The woman went on.

"It says you are getting a surgery today. Have you ever received this before?"

"I guess I am. I won't be awake to know about it though. Let's go," Jerry exclaimed as he turned to his father looking for a party.

"That's not what she asked you," Dominick sternly replied. "Try again."

"I'm sorry, nurse. I am just really excited to go under anesthesia. No, I have never had surgery before," Jerry said formally.

"It's fine. I remember I felt the same way you did my first time getting it," she responded. "It is truly incredible. I love it."

The party that Jerry was searching for just occurred in his head.

She led the family to a very large and open area. Unlike the waiting room, there were no walls dividing patients. Each patient would lie in a box sectioned off by a curtain.

She pointed to the back corner.

"The gown is supposed to be open in the back," she said while handing Jerry a package.

She left without any more instructions.

"What?" Jerry asked his parents.

"The gown always opens in the back," Dominick replied.

"No," Jerry continued. "How are there wooden walls dividing patients in the waiting room, but just sheets of paper here. I mean I am going to be naked in a second."

"They don't do nothing without a reason bro," Dominick shrugged and looked out the window. Jerry joined him.

Through the small window, they were met with a brick wall from the next building. The wall forced him back into the room—left with only one way to escape.

Someone appeared alongside the curtain a couple minutes later.

"Can I come in?" the voice questioned as there was no door to knock on.

A woman emerged. She was slightly older than Jerry's parents, but not elderly. She wore a mask that stretched across her face. The mask alongside her long greasy hair helped cover many wrinkles. She needed a shower.

"Hello! My name is Doctor P. I am your anesthesiologist," she charmed. "How are you guys today?"

"Hanging in there," Dominick responded. "I think my son is excited to see you."

Doctor P. looked Jerry in the eyes.

Jerry's mind wandered off as he found her in Hollywood. This woman pushed Britney Spears off the red carpet and nobody batted an eye. She was the most beautiful supermodel around.

"Jerry?" She chuckled.

That one word brought him back to his encaged corner.

"Sorry. I'm here. I heard you knock people out," Jerry tried to be as friendly as possible.

"Well, I wouldn't say it like that," Doctor P. chuckled as she looked at Dominick and Ella. "I put people under anesthesia to make surgeries easier."

"I know. I know. I read all about it. I am so excited. I can't wait for you to knock me out," Jerry sounded like a child.

"Doctor P.," Dominick started. "He is incredibly scared of needles. He always freaks out. Upstairs, on floor 9, they call him the 'hulk' because he is big and turns green."

"No way," Doctor P. squealed out as she laughed way too hard.

"But he is not nervous whatsoever to be here right now. He believes you'll knock him out and he won't even have to see a needle. You're like a hero to him right now," Dominick added.

"Oh boy, here goes nothing," Doctor P. looked down and then at Jerry.

"You are a big kid. You're basically a little man. In order to knock you out I need to put the anesthesia through an IV. It's a big hassle to give enough anesthesia under the kid masks, then transfer to an IV. I don't want to do it."

Jerry sank into his bed as his father spoke.

"This may not matter, but I just want to let you know. He is 14."

"Yeah, I know, but he's one big 14-year-old," She took a breath and looked at Dominick.

"How could something be so big and so afraid of a tiny little needle," she said pointing at Jerry like he was just an object.

Another woman with a lanyard around her neck came in. She had a pop-up table on wheels. As she pushed it closer, Jerry caught a glimpse of a green cap.

Jerry felt the walls closing in on him. Each second passing was valuable. He knew he must do something.

"Doctor P.," Jerry desperately started. "I was so excited today. Out of all the times I have had to come here, I thought this would be the best one. Please don't do this to me."

Doctor P.'s attitude didn't budge.

"I'm sorry but we have to do this. Help me, help you. The quicker we do this, the quicker I can put you under."

The nurse approached the bedside. She ripped a seal holding the tubing together.

Jerry felt his projected sorrow vanish in the empty air.

Why would you beg Jerry, he thought to himself. *You are not a victim. Try something else…logic, logic, logic.*

"*Help me, help you.*" Jerry sat up strongly.

Doctor P. became motionless.

"Getting this IV in will be a fight. Would you rather the hassle of having to transfer the anesthesia or fighting me. Why not just help me out? Also, I will only give you one specific vein. Nothing else. If you give me the mask first, you can choose any vein you want."

Doctor P. remained still for a moment, giving Jerry the opportunity to throw one more line in.

"Please knock me out. It would make everything easier for both of us. We're on the same team here."

"Give me one second," Doctor P. shut the curtain behind her and the nurse.

Jerry felt their presence as the pop-up table stayed next to his bed. For only a split second, the empty tiles surrounding this table gave him the opportunity to breathe.

"Fair play, fair play," Dominick smirked as he looked down. His hands took refuge in his pockets.

"You adjusted quickly there. Let's just see if it works. Regardless, that was good. I'm impressed," Ella said, standing up very straight.

Though the nurse was in close proximity to the pop-up table, he realized the curtain separated the two different dimensions. The nurse would have to break through that cement barrier to reach him.

Just as he regained the ability to speak again, the two women moved past the wall and went no further than a couple of feet.

"I'll put you under first," Doctor P. started in a monotone voice. "We need to work with patients, not against them. I'll give you the mask, then do everything needed."

The nurse rolled the frightening table to the other side of the curtain. The two of them started to make their way out, until Doctor P. froze.

"Also, you're a very brave kid," Her face lit up. "Never lose that."

Tool Acquired: Collaboration

APPLYING THE TOOL

Doctor P. looked like a villain. She wasn't. She was just doing her job.

The people trying to help you won't always feel like it in the moment. Some definitely don't make it feel that way. But it is.

A coach pushing you, a teacher failing you, a doctor poking you—they are all in your corner. The sooner you embrace that, the sooner you stop wasting your energy on the wrong battle.

Use logic and never be a victim.

Jerry wasn't the brightest when it comes to history, but he watched a couple of videos about D-Day. He didn't know everything, but he knew it was horrid. In his mind, he called every chemotherapy date a D-Day. He considered it like something he just had to serve.

The day before a D-Day his forehead would always be dripping sweat at 11:50. Whether it was countless push-ups, holding squatting positions, or his ab workout, he wanted to get every workout in for the next day. He couldn't just allow his power to be "zapped" out of him.

He thanked a higher power that today was his last D-Day.

Even though he was a Baltimore Orioles fan, he threw on his Pittsburgh Pirates shirt the next morning. Every other D-Day he had worn the shirt, so he wanted to keep the trend.

Looking down on his shirt wasn't the word "pirates," rather just a massive "P." To him, that "P" stood for one of his favorite words of all time: prevail.

As his family stepped out of the parking garage, he looked down and nodded.

Yeah. I will.

He took a moment.

Not today, but one day.

Jerry's eyes felt heavy from the bags under them. He looked like he had just come off a night shift. In some ways, he did—but he worked for something greater than money.

He sleepwalked his way into the same elevator that started everything. Jerry threw his finger to the number 9. It started blinking. It was like a Fourth of July firework show. However, the sleep crust in his eyes covered some of the magic.

The door opened and Jerry was met with the same color paintings. Nothing was unusual as he was ready to take on the day.

Turning the corner, he saw the front desk lady standing. Her head was tilted to the side. She wore a massive smile with her hands interlocked in front of her chest.

Jerry's eyebrows raised slightly. He was too tired to even worry about it…then it hit him.

BOTTOM OF THE NINTH. YOU GOT THIS, read a poster. The words were written on a beautiful drawn baseball field outlined by flimsy LED lights.

Tape held it together.

His aunt held it up.

His uncle and aunt from Pennsylvania had been waiting by the front desk. Due to the lengthy distance between them and the hospital, they also had to pull a midnight shift.

Aunt Gianna was on Dominick's side of the family. Still, Ella immediately ran towards her. They left no space between their bodies as they grappled onto each other.

Jerry's hands circled and surrounded his eyes as if he was looking through a window. However, he wasn't looking into a window, rather his father's chest. A single droplet of water slowly fell from his eyes.

Uncle Jayson held a blank face through the whirling emotions around him. This stillness made Jerry gravitate towards him first.

"Thank you," Jerry said as they shook hands.

"Anytime kiddo," Uncle Jayson responded with a smirk.

As Jerry let go of Uncle Jayson's hand, he saw a train approaching him. Aunt Gianna was a snowman in 100-degree weather as she melted into Jerry's arms.

"I love you," Aunt Gianna sobbed.

"I love you too," Jerry held himself strongly.

As normal lobby customs started to reoccur, Jerry never spoke.

*They drove all the way here from middle of nowhere Pennsylvani*a, Jerry's thoughts stunned him. *It is 8 in the morning. Besides, I am not doing anything. I am going to go lay on a bed.*

"Your room is ready," said softly by the front desk lady.

After an eternity, the two groups said their goodbyes and parted ways. Ella carried the sign.

Walking towards the back, they were stuck behind a massive painting truck. It moved the speed of a snail.

"Ugh," Jerry said as he looked to the ceiling. It appeared as if he was carrying a weight.

"You alright there?" Dominick asked worriedly.

"I'm fine," Jerry answered shortly as he clenched his fist.

Why in the world did I get a sign? I'm not doing anything.

They were directed into their specific room past an office filled with young nurses. They all waved to Jerry as he passed by.

He felt a fire growing inside of him.

Jerry lay down in his bed and lifted his head up.

There was a white board underneath a TV. The whiteboard had a checklist of the upcoming steps in order.

He calmly read the word "IV" twice. He was ready as he had seen this on prior D-Days.

Next to the whiteboard was a handmade sign outlined by flimsy LED lights. Jerry threw his head back into the pillow. His eyelids shut.

"Hey Jerry," Ella asked normally. "Did you see the trade the Yankees just made?"

"Yes it was very cool," Jerry said quickly. His eyes remained shut.

"No, no, no. Stop. Something is wrong here. I know it," Dominick said. "We have been through a lot and I've never seen you act like this. You're acting like a jerk."

"No I'm not. Just shut up. Okay?" Jerry said shortly. He turned facing the wall in his bed.

"Something is wrong. I am not just going to let my son suffer," Dominick instantly responded.

"Everything is fine," Jerry started. He looked over his shoulder at his father. Then, he caught a glimpse of the LED lights and back at Dominick. “Are you really going to fight with me as I lay on my chemotherapy bed? Come on bro.”

Jerry turned back around with his face to the wall. His mind needed to be extinguished from the fire.

“Where there’s smoke, there’s fire,” Dominick whispered.

Dominick believed, and had always taught Jerry, that the first step of fixing any problem is identifying it. Like a lion searching for food, Dominick relentlessly looked for the problem.

“We’ve done this before and I've never seen this. What is different about this time?” Dominick spoke to Ella.

Jerry didn’t hear this statement. He was in his own world.

Dominick thought deeply about everything that occurred today. He put his head down.

As his eyes stared at the floor, a couple tiles were a little brighter than others.

“Turn the poster around Ella,” Dominick announced. “And turn off the lights too.”

He took a second and then continued.

"Jerry, I know this isn't you. Just forget about the poster. It was supposed to be a nice gesture. It seemed to have helped everyone else, but you."

Jerry turned around in fire.

"I hate it. It is terrible. The whole thing is just flawed."

"Explain," Dominick asked.

"It says "*I GOT THIS*."" Jerry sat up. "I don't have anything. I am just lying on a bed like a mannequin. I just have to put my faith in them—that's the only thing I can control."

Jerry took a second.

"I'm sorry," Jerry looked down. "I just hate how the poster puts the pressure on me, the pressure is on the doctors."

He continued. The more he spoke, the more his fire morphed into something beneficial.

"Seeing Mom run towards it like a child made me furious. She embraced the wrong side. I believe that mindset is terrible," Jerry looked at her. "I hope you can actually understand that nothing is on me. The doctors do it all. I put all my faith in them and the man above. How do you think I've stayed mentally fine this whole time?"

The walls stopped closing in on Jerry, rather they pushed back. His flame was no longer burning his house down, rather heating up his food.

Dominick and Ella were left without words. The silence prolonged for a while, until Jerry reached for the TV remote. He put on a baseball game which helped soften the

room.

Suddenly two nurses walked in. Jerry smiled as he recognized both of their faces.

"Hey Jerry," said Kiara in a charming voice. "I was happy to see your name on my paper today."

Kiara settled in.

"I also brought a friend with me today. Her name is Jessica. She's the best."

"Stop that," Jessica smiled. "Of course I know Jerry. He's the best. He's just a little scared of needles."

"What? Me? Scared of needles, no way," Jerry chuckled. "I promise I won't punch either of you guys today."

Both of their expressions brightened.

Jessica had left the room.

"How are you feeling today?" Kiara questioned. "Also, I see you got your Pirates shirt on. I feel like you wear that every time I see you."

"Feeling amazing. And I guess the shirt is a coincidence," Jerry said aloud. Inside, he knew it wasn't.

Jessica returned with a very similar pop-up table.

The bags under Jerry's eyes had totally vanished as he saw a whole sheet of green caps.

Jessica popped two out.

Even though he didn't like to see the two green caps emerge from the paper, he realized it could have been a lot worse.

"I'm sorry, but you know what time it is," Kiara spoke in a friendly tone. "Don't worry. Jessica does this in her sleep."

"Please only do this one," Jerry pointed to a very specific forearm vein.

"Ok but we need two IVs today. Are you sure you want them both in the same vein?" Jessica questioned.

"Yes, I am more than sure," Jerry slammed his eyes shut. "Just go and don't tell me."

Although the nurses didn't even place the tourniquet, Jerry's mind went off. His breathing became very fast and loud. His body became a brick wall. But unfortunately, Jerry had gained enough experience to know what to do.

He understood that if the nurses couldn't get the IV in, he would just get poked more times. He also knew that his body being stiff didn't matter as long as he could relax the arm—which is exactly what he did.

"You're killing it, Jerry," Kiara said happily. "We're almost done."

"You're a rockstar," Jessica added. Kiara followed that up.

"He really is a rockstar. I would even say superstar."

Jerry's mind cultivated a million thoughts as he questioned reality.

WHAT? I'm not a rockstar. I'm laying here like a lab rat while they try to save my life. I just don't understand. I mean superstar, too. Doesn't even make sense.

Kiara's face beamed as she snapped Jerry back into the room.

"All done. You did it."

Yeah okay. I, myself, did it. The kid that sat there with my eyes shut did it alright. Jerry thought as he smiled.

"Thank you Jessica for coming," Kiara used her hands to present her to Jerry, like she was a prize on a game show. "I told you she's the best."

Jessica added to the delusion.

"Oh please. He's the amazing one," Jessica said while smiling intensely at Jerry. "That's why I came here."

From the bottom of their hearts, the family genuinely thanked the two women as they exited the room.

Jerry looked at his parents and spoke.

"Thank you for taking me to this hospital. They're rockstars."

Tool Acquired: Trust

APPLYING THE TOOL

Don't fall for the flashy poster with lights. Stay true to the real strength. This power is not flashy. It doesn't need an audience.

Strength is quiet. One part of it stems from putting your trust in the right places, allowing you to escape from a lack of control.

Turn your poster around.

Dominick had always pushed Jerry about being on time. He always claimed that if you arrive right before the bell, you are late. Although Jerry never saw the true value of this concept, he always was prepared at the start time—not to arrive at it.

This idea led to Jerry always maintaining perfect attendance all throughout his life. He never wanted to make his father disappointed, especially on something so easy. However, his medical condition shattered this record.

Jerry's family had worked intensely on minimizing the number of absences in school. Dominick always tried to schedule Jerry's many doctor appointments on weekends and holidays. Ella had to rearrange her work hours due to Jerry not being allowed on a school bus. The tight indoor space would not mix well with Jerry's compromised immune system.

In addition to Dominick and Ella's incredible efforts, Jerry pushed himself to be in that building. He even came to school the day after receiving chemotherapy—regardless of how the chemicals made his stomach feel. Jerry hated to have to leave his seat empty.

During baseball season, the extremeness of Jerry's actions increased. There were multiple times where Jerry served his time in the hospital in the morning, and played baseball in the afternoon. One time, he had to quickly excuse himself from practice for his virtual doctor's appointment about his radiation. Then he normally worked his way back in like nothing had happened.

• • •

After missing multiple days of school, Jerry needed to hand in his doctor's notes. Before school one day, Jerry separated from his friends as he went to the attendance lady with a stack of envelopes.

The weight of all of these papers slowed Jerry down on his walk to the lady. Jerry wasn't able to completely wrap his hand around this brick.

The main office's wall was made completely out of glass. As he walked towards the room, Jerry could already catch a glimpse of the lady. An unpleasant feeling shot up his spine.

The lady's hair color matched the night sky. Its darkness matched her smeared, sloppy makeup. Her face stared sternly at her mounted computer as her fingers aggressively hit each key. Everything about this lady screamed the word "negativity."

A picture framed in front of her desk froze Jerry. It was the lady holding a small child.

Who would marry this lady? She looks like a ball of anger. Jerry thought as he pulled the big glass door.

However, Jerry didn't believe in judging someone on appearances so he approached her with an open mind.

"Hello, I am here to drop off my doctor's notes," Jerry said as he handed the encyclopedia of papers over to her.

"One second. Can't you see I'm doing something?" the lady said with a touch of anger.

"Sorry," Jerry softly said.

After a brief moment, she continued.

"Can I help you?"

"Yes. I am here to drop off my doctor's notes," Jerry spoke politely.

"Give me them," the lady said quickly. "This is terrible."

"What's wrong?" Jerry asked.

"You are missing too much school. Your appointments should be on non-school days," The lady's touch of anger grew slightly.

"What do you mean? Am I going to get detention? I mean all of these absences should be excused," Jerry said with an inflection in his voice. He was surprised that the conversation was occurring.

"In terms of policy you are okay, they are excused. But it is no excuse to be missing this much school. Your education is very important," The lady's anger was now present in her voice.

Jerry held his ground.

"I'm sorry but my health is more important. I wish I didn't have to miss this much."

"Don't argue with me. I am the adult here. Therefore, you don't get the ability to go back at me," her voice was hostile.

"I'm sorry I am not trying to argue with you. I'm just"

"ZIP IT," the lady snapped. "You don't know everything."

Jerry's palms opened towards the ceiling. His eyebrows caved in.

"Don't give me that attitude. Leave before I write you up," She was in full attack mode.

"But I didn't even…" Jerry tried to start as he took steps back.

"DOOR," she pointed towards the hallways.

Jerry's mouth was stuck wide open as he silently exited the room. His spine was right.

I guess the rumors about her are true after all.

Going throughout the day, Jerry replayed that whole interaction in his head. Although his fist clenched every time he thought about it, he couldn't stop.

In between classes, he didn't shake as many hands as usual. Jerry's lit up face seemed dimmer. The tone of the day wasn't the same—he needed help.

Dominick ran through the same routine every time Jerry came home from school.

"How was your day? What did you learn?" Dominick asked normally. He then switched to a zombie voice.

"Boring. Nothing."

This sequence always got a chuckle and hug out of Jerry. However, Jerry cut him off today.

"Actually, I want your old-man wisdom. I'm kind of at a loss here."

"Oh yeah. Let's go," Dominick responded with a laugh. He then distinctively pointed at his forehead.

"You know I got a lot of that. Ok but seriously, what's up?"

"Ok, so you know how I had to drop off all my doctor's notes today. The lady was the biggest jerk ever. She was angry as soon as I opened my mouth," Jerry started, but Dominick cut him off.

"Oh no. You probably gave the lady an attitude. If I know you, this is definitely your fault," Dominick said with a smile.

"Dad, I promise you. This time I swear it wasn't me. She is like 100 times meaner than Mom. Just looking at her, you can see all the anger. I tried to be extra nice and she yelled at me for missing school. I told her that my health comes before school and that I wish I didn't have to miss. Then she yelled at me to not argue with her," Jerry was undeniably speaking with passion.

"Ok, I believe you. There are many bad apples out there. Don't worry, I know exactly how to fix this one. But let me ask you. How did you feel after the conversation, like throughout the day?" Dominick responded.

"Terrible," Jerry exclaimed. "The day didn't feel like a normal one."

Dominick smirked. He knew he had complete control here.

"Exactly. That is why you can't engage with fire—you'll catch a spark and burn on your own time. The funny part is she knew this. She said 'don't argue with her,' she was right. Take this in a broader sense. When somebody insults you, what is their goal?"

"To make you feel bad," Jerry responded hesitantly then Dominick continued.

"Yes. Therefore, if you do actually feel bad then you are letting them win. If you walk away unfazed then you win. I'm not saying the lady was insulting you, but it sounds like she was reflecting her own anger onto you. You must never take that."

"But how do I not take that? I mean they are throwing it at me," Jerry quickly asked.

"Just because someone throws something at you doesn't mean you have to catch it. You know a lot about that being a baseball catcher," Dominick smiled and continued.

"But seriously, comments can simply deflect right off of you. Never internalize someone else's negative projections of themselves. Let me leave you with this Jerry: It takes a fool to argue with a fool." [2]

"Wow. You are smarter than you look," Jerry laughed. "That is exactly what I needed to hear."

"Wait, though. One more thing," Dominick raised his voice. "We can talk about this all day, but nothing actually matters unless you embrace it. Please use it next time. I don't want to see anyone shake you from being yourself."

"Oh don't worry Dad, I will."

About two months later, that moment had arrived. Jerry had ingrained his father's philosophy into his life. He was ready.

Jerry carried a similar stack of envelopes as he walked past the glass hallway. His head was back and his shoulders were up.

Let's do this, Jerry thought to himself as he pulled open the glass door.

"Hello. I am here to drop off my doctor's notes," Jerry said as a huge smile grew on his face.

Dark eye shadow completely surrounded the lady's eyes. She made direct eye contact with Jerry. However, he wasn't going to break this time.

"What did I tell you the last time?" A rude tone overcame this woman's voice.

"I'm not really sure," Jerry said happily as he dropped his papers on her desk. "I would stay and talk but I have to go."

Jerry took a couple of steps towards the door as the voice snapped.

"How dare you. Don't blow me off. Come back here."

Her dark eye shadow turned blood red.

"How dare I what?" Jerry turned around. He spoke at a normal volume, a bit firmly. "Respectfully, I don't owe you a conversation. I don't have to explain myself to you. I'm going to leave now. Have a great day."

The lady raised her voice and it began to tremble.

"But I am an adult."

"And I am a teenager. Have a great day," Jerry smiled as he left the room feeling like his normal, happy self.

Tool Acquired: Selective Detachment

2-A quotation from Mark Twain.

APPLYING THE TOOL

If you are willing to listen to ideas, you are already something greater than the Cranky Attendance Ladies. Never allow parasites to drain you.

Jerry smiled and walked out that door. Not due to innocence, but understanding.

Walk out yours.

Jerry rolled out of bed at a relatively normal hour, 7 A.M. He had a whole day of scans ahead of him. At 11:55 the day prior, he was devouring a jar of peanut butter for the calories. Not only did the calories help fill his stomach, they helped Jerry fuel something more important: his mind.

Jerry took pride in the act of doing meaningful work way past normal hours, whether morning or night. These times helped construct him for the long-run, even though some days his eyes felt like dumbbells.

Soon after, midnight had passed and he lost his ability to eat.

The next morning. The family had gotten in the car as they took off for the hospital. The ride always was a struggle. Between going over a massive river, fighting with New York City traffic, or dealing with the parking companies, nothing was ever fluid. Jerry never fully comprehended that one way on the George Washington bridge was about 15 dollars—let alone the tolls for the parking garage.

Although the commute was terrible, it had to happen. Jerry needed to serve his time. No inconvenience would ever stop that.

The family dropped their car off in a parking garage a couple blocks from the hospital. After that, they walked on the sidewalks of New York City.

Jerry felt his steps were different from everyone else's. To Jerry, the average pedestrian was a late soldier. They rushed through their neighborhoods hyper fixated on arriving at the destination. Countless do this without ever realizing the magic of the buildings surrounding them.

Through the ocean of blind people, Jerry spotted a hotdog stand nearby.

"Dad," Jerry sounded like a five-year old. "Can we please get hotdogs when we are done? Pretty Please with a cherry on top."

"Of course, you know the answer is yes. You don't have to do all that," Dominick laughed.

"Fire. Let's go!" Jerry said as he practically skipped into the building.

Not only would Jerry eat anything possible, but now he could have one of his favorite foods. Now, Jerry just wanted the scans to end as he couldn't wait for the hot dogs. It had even taken his mind off the fact that he was about to get an IV.

Jerry sat in the waiting room. Unlike every other time, he was excited to hear his name today.

"Jerry," called a woman.

Immediately, Jerry pushed the floor down as he jumped out of his seat. His hoodie flew off of him as he aggressively propelled his body towards her.

"Let's do this. Needle me," Jerry said with courage.

Jerry took this sense of strength all the way to the chair. He very quickly threw out his forearm and shut his eyes. He pictured running out of the building and riding a hotdog into the sunset.

Even though he was moving fast, Jerry's reputation stayed. Two nurses held him down, Dominick lightly placed an ice pack behind his neck, and Jerry bit his shirt as his toes tapped the floor intensely. He honestly still needed it.

The nurses celebrated after they quickly got the IV into the only vein Jerry allowed them to.

"Thank you guys," Jerry said as he sprung up and held his arm at a 90-degree angle against his body.

Before he could take even a step, he felt the spring had a recoil effect.

His head felt like a feather as he tried to hear his nurses. Jerry tried to understand what the nurses were saying, but he couldn't.

"Actually just give me a minute," Jerry chuckled.

After a moment, his hearing came back to him and he heard a nurse.

"Of course. Do you need us to wheelchair you out?" One nurse responded.

"No, I will be okay. Thank you though," a smile grew on Jerry's face.

"Are you sure Jerry? I don't want you to walk to the waiting room again and then complain about seeing stars like the last time," Dominick butted in.

"Well everything would be better if I had sugar in me," Jerry normally replied. "But whatever, it's okay."

The nurse Jerry had recognized left the room in a hurry. Remaining alongside Jerry were his parents and this young female nurse.

Jerry had never seen her before. She was blonde and no older than 25. Her charm gleamed past her lanyard that was pinned with every cartoon character imaginable. During the IV placement, however, she seemed to follow the other nurse's lead.

This blonde girl opened her mouth.

"I have to give you this drink. It is for your scans. And then after that you can eat as much as you want," she said with way too much energy in her voice.

Dominick froze and his hands moved as he talked.

"Really? Honestly, he has been going through chemotherapy so we haven't had scans in a while. It's weird because he can eat then, but I thought he can't eat before his scans."

"Nope, Nope, Nopidity Nope. He can eat," the blonde nurse responded. Her words didn't feel heavy, but her personality did the lifting.

"Oh, wow okay. That is awesome. Yeah, my bad I guess I was mistaken," Dominick replied looking down.

Jerry's mind was stunned. Jerry's stomach was ecstatic.

The family walked back to the waiting room and Jerry immediately started talking.

"Well, you heard the nurse. Can I eat something?" Jerry asked energetically.

"Jerry, man, I have a bad feeling about this. I don't remember you ever being able to eat. But I think you were able to during chemotherapy. I don't know. Maybe this waiting room is just driving me crazy," Dominick responded while his head moved left and right.

Jerry took a breath as his stomach cried for help.

"Yeah, I feel the same way. But we just had a nurse tell us we're wrong."

Dominick cut him off.

"Yeah but she didn't seem like the most credible doctor in this building."

"Well, this is literally the number 1 hospital in the world. Even though she appeared a little crazy, she does work here," Jerry said.

"I guess you are right," Dominick looked to his side. "Ella, what do you think?"

Ella answered in a calm, rational tone. Her voice gave off a trustworthy impression.

"I can see where both of you are coming from. But it has been a long time since we've had to get a scan. And we just had a medical professional back Jerry's point up."

"Alright," Dominick started. "Maybe he is allowed to eat during the chemotherapy and the scans. I'm probably wrong. Do you have anything in your purse Jerry could eat right now?"

Ella reached into the depths of her bag. She searched until her hand felt something promising. She pulled it up and presented it to the world.

It was Jerry's favorite granola bar. But something was off about this specific one. The bar was barely larger than Jerry's middle finger. The packaging even had colors that seemed strange.

The words: *50 PERCENT REDUCED SUGAR*, were written in the discoloration.

"This is all I have," Ella said.

"I would say you can go to the pantry, but we are leaving now. Just take the bar and later I can grab something quick at the cafeteria downstairs," Dominick spoke confidently.

Jerry's jaw dropped when those words came out of his father's mouth.

"Ok, I'll happily eat it. It's better than nothing," Jerry's arm reached to grab the snack from his mother.

Even though his stomach had reached out for it, his mind didn't. This collision led to Jerry's hand slowly outstretching through the air.

Jerry's fingers eventually surrounded the entire tiny bar. He pulled it towards himself and gave it a big hug. He then was ready to eat it.

Jerry stopped for a second as the bar was in between his lips. He turned off his thoughts and sank his teeth in—ripping the bar in half. This explosion had released sugar all throughout his body.

Dominick spoke while Jerry cherished the party his tastebuds were having.

"Ok. I'm really surprised we were able to do that, but hopefully it helps. Now you got a little something in you, we need to go downstairs. I kind of forgot which floor though."

Jerry and Ella waited by the elevators while Dominick got directions from the front desk lady.

The elevator dropped its passengers, while Jerry's stomach had dropped on him.

Uncertainty shot all through his body. It flowed through his IV, hit the green cap, and was back through his body.

Jerry tried multiple times to flashback to the nurse's charm, but nothing helped. These sensations were running wild.

Dominick came back with a piece of paper. He became the captain of the ship as he directed his family through the hospital.

They went down to floor 5 and Dominick kept walking in unpredictable paths. Although Jerry had been through many scans, he didn't recognize even one drop of paint on the wall.

There was always massive construction going on at this hospital. Whether it was decorating the walls or developing new chemotherapies, they were always up to something.

Eventually, the family stumbled upon something promising. There was a little front desk on the way to a waiting room.

Dominick stopped at the desk, while Jerry and Ella went on to explore.

Jerry pushed the abnormally wide double-doors and was met with a large opening. The walls were lined with windows. There were plenty of chairs and two big-screen TVs.

Jerry and Ella walked to the back to sit by themselves.

As Jerry tried to sit down, he couldn't help but look through a window.

He was met by the energy of the city. Being on the fifth floor, he had a perfect overhead view of the creatures. He marveled at the many pieces all coexisting together.

After a couple of minutes, Dominick poked his head in the room and called for Jerry. Unfortunately, the doctors limited the amount of people in the next room due to radiation.

“I’ll be okay,” Jerry whispered as he kissed Ella goodbye.

Dominick was standing with a nurse. She directed them into an incredibly tiny room. It was broken off into two sections by half of a wooden wall. She seated them on the far side and took off without many words.

A couple minutes later, another nurse walked into the room. Jerry felt like she was a late soldier as she rushed everything. After speedrunning through an introduction, she ran out to get a pop-up table.

Although this pop-up table looked like all the others, it was different. It held no tubing or green caps. Rather, there was a miniature table cloth underneath something strange.

Jerry stared at the black object trying to figure out what it was. He naturally flash backed.

• • •

"Are you sure we are allowed to do this?" 9-year-old Jerry asked his best friend, Lucas.

"Of course we can," Lucas responded. "We are his friends. It will be funny. Let's go together."

Lucas and Jerry were eyeing down the mansion of their friend. On the doorstep was a massive Frankenstein with a huge cauldron. The cauldron had a sign that read TAKE TWO.

Jerry caught a glimpse of this sign.

"Lucas, wait," Jerry's stomach was starting to twist. "It says to only take two pieces of candy."

Lucas pulled up his mask to read the sign.

"No it doesn't. It says take two. Let's go take two bagfuls. We do have two bags," Lucas said confidently.

"Ok," Jerry gulped. "You lead the way."

The two boys giggled all the way up the stairs until they reached the candy bowl.

Jerry and Lucas ransacked this huge cauldron as quickly as they could. Their minds had lost all situational awareness.

A tall door opened up right alongside them.

"Guys!" the man screamed. "You can't do that."

The two boys recognized this man. Behind this strong figure, was a boy around their age. He was pointing and dying of laughter.

"Put the candy back now!" the man exclaimed and turned to Jerry.

"Jerry, I know your mother. I am calling her right now."

Jerry's eyes had dropped a couple of tears as the man turned to Lucas.

"Take off your mask right now."

Lucas immediately took off. He sprinted across the street into someone's backyard.

The man froze for a second. Then he returned his attention back to Jerry.

"Please don't call her. Please," Jerry shrieked as tears fell down his cheeks.

"I have to. What you did is very wrong," the man replied.

"I am so sorry. I didn't want to do it. He convinced me," Jerry cried as he pointed at the house he ran off to.

"That doesn't make it right," the man responded.

Jerry took a seat as the river had officially rushed down his face. He was a sitting duck waiting for Ella.

• • •

I got it. It's a cauldron.

Jerry gulped.

Not again.

A lid was on the cauldron. Jerry watched some steam squeeze right by this lid. The pot itself was elevated with thick legs. The majority of gases escaped this way and spread all over the room.

The lady had zero patience as she quickly asked one question.

“You haven’t had food since midnight, right?”

The lady asked the question as if it was just protocol. She was already putting on her gloves ready to make the next move.

“Actually, I had a granola bar about an hour ago. The nurse told me I could,” Jerry spoke softly.

“Ok never mind then. We can’t do this right now,” her hurry slowed as she talked at a normal pace. “You guys have two options. You can either wait 4 hours or you can come back tomorrow. Your choice.”

“What!?” Dominick raised his voice. “The nurse upstairs said we were allowed. She was adamant."

“Sorry sir, but there is nothing we can do here. The sugar in the food will give us inaccurate results with this,” she said and pointed at the cauldron.

"Oh my god," Jerry looked at his empty stomach and then back at the nurse. "But the bar had 50 percent reduced sugar. It was tiny. It was like I had eaten nothing."

"I am sorry but it still has some sugar. There is nothing we can do. You guys can just come back tomorrow," the nurse replied.

"No, not really. This trip is incredibly hard for us. I guess we will wait four hours," Dominick said with annoyance in his voice.

"Ok. You can leave this room now and go wherever. Just return to the front desk in four hours. We will do a fingerstick test to confirm his sugar levels are ready, but we should be fine," the nurse said in a monotone voice.

Without looking back, she had left the room with her cauldron.

Dominick and Jerry looked at each other for a moment without words.

Jerry gulped as he felt nothing in his stomach.

"I am going to be even hungrier than without the stupid bar," Jerry said on the verge of a breakdown.

"Well, Jerry," Dominick took a breath. "We should have trusted our instincts."

Jerry took a breath as his stomach rumbled. Each hunger pain reminded him of something greater. He spoke through his guilt.

"The nurse wasn't wrong. I was."

"But the nurse did tell us we could," Dominick replied.

Jerry took a deep breath.

"That doesn't make it right."

Tool Acquired: Direction

APPLYING THE TOOL

You could be absolutely starving. You could have a nurse tell you that it is okay. You could trick others into believing it. Everything could seem perfect, except for a little feeling.

That's your sign.

Don't live with the weight.

Never eat the granola bar.

Unfortunately, Jerry found himself in a familiar corner. His space was surrounded by curtains. He didn't have his usual clothes on, rather a gown that was open in the back.

"Hey Jerry," Dominick said hesitantly. "I didn't want you to work yourself up about coming today. That is why I didn't tell you this. But we are probably going to get started soon and I need to."

"Tell me what," Jerry's positivity turned into caution.

"Well, I loved how you acted at the time of your last surgery and today, so please don't let that change. But Doctor P is out today," Dominick said smoothly.

"Oh ok," Jerry held his normal self. "That's no big deal. I'll just talk to the new doctor."

"You see Jerry, that was the problem. Ella and I reached out to her on the portal. We wanted to do your request early for you to get everything sorted beforehand. We said similar things that you said to Doctor P, but this doctor refused to budge even a little."

Dominick raised his tone. "We don't even get the ability to meet her."

"I don't want to meet her. She seems very mean," Ella chimed in.

"Yeah, I agree with Ella," Dominick started and then looked down. "I am sorry about not telling you. I just hate to see your mind work against you."

Jerry sunk into his hospital bed.

"It's okay," Jerry said as he shut his eyes. He hoped he was invisible.

He didn't think he was, but his suspicions were confirmed when a woman walked in.

She was probably in her forties with short blonde hair. A lanyard wrapped around her neck read the words: CHILD LIFE SPECIALIST.

The woman also wore a mask that angled out to a point. Jerry saw a lot of pointed masks during COVID-19, but this was different. The mask had the traditional angled structure but vertically, making her look like a platypus.

The lady checked off a box on a clipboard with her pen and started the conversation.

"How are you today?" the woman spoke with a touch of charm.

"Ehh," Jerry started but Dominick jumped in.

"Not very well. He is incredibly scared of IVs. The last time they put him under anesthesia beforehand, but they can't do it today."

"There is nothing to be afraid of with IVs. Trust me," the woman replied.

In the same breath she easily asked a heavy question like it was nothing.

"So, you're here for a port right?"

Jerry's heart dropped.

"No, I believe it is just a biopsy today," Dominick said inquisitively.

"Oh, you are right. I am in the wrong room. Sorry. Well, I got something for you," The woman said as she went behind the curtains.

Jerry's hands were visibly shaking. His pounding heart was audible.

Within a minute, the woman with the duck-bill appeared. She held something in her hands.

"Here. Let me show you," the woman spoke as she presented an unusual object.

Jerry got a glimpse of a green cap attached to a clear tube.

"NO. NO," Jerry screamed as his head shot away from her. His palms instantly pointed towards the object like he was Iron Man.

"I am not giving you an IV. This is just a demonstration to show you how it works. It's not scary. Let me show you," the woman persisted.

"I said no," Jerry said as he was visibly twisting and turning in the bed.

Even though Jerry reacted strongly, she stood there. She stayed insistent about showing this demonstration. Ella and Dominick both stepped in front of her, becoming a wall.

Instantly, the platypus ran off with Jerry's calm.

So much for a Child Life Specialist.

"Can I come in?" sounded a voice outside the curtain fifteen minutes after the storm.

A middle-aged nurse had entered the cage. She beamed at Jerry.

"I am here to give you your IV."

Jerry barely even looked back at her. Dominick knew he needed to step in.

Dominick gave her the whole run-down. He talked about how Jerry always had two nurses, how Jerry convinced the anesthesiologist to knock him out first, and how he got the 'hulk' nickname.

It was as if his words had hit a brick wall.

"I don't care. We'll be fine. I've been doing this a long time. Besides, I can already tell he likes me," the lady spoke with a high amount of energy.

Jerry looked away.

"Oh come on. We are going to do great together. This will be fun," the nurse said running over in the direction Jerry was looking.

"No, it won't," Jerry responded looking her straight in the eyes.

The lady immediately shied away and hid behind her pop-up table. There was no way Jerry would break that eye contact first. Her fake positivity turned Jerry's face red.

"Alright, well you at least got to work with her," Dominick tried to break up the tension.

"Unfortunately," Jerry responded as he shook his head and let out a deep breath. "I'm sorry. I just really hate this and another lady came in here before just to scare me."

"Well, it is okay. I understand. Let's just get this over with," the nurse replied.

Jerry felt a sense of relief. He loved hearing that statement from her. He believed that the nurse really did have a "human" side.

The nurse went next to Jerry. She took out an alcohol pad and started to clean his arm.

Although Jerry still had no color on his face, he burst out into laughter. The broken laughs persisted as he winced throughout the whole interaction.

As the nurse picked up her needle, she lost her touch.

"Someone is in a good mood," her face grew an irking smile.

"Yes. I am just so happy to be here," Jerry responded sarcastically. His hysteria prevented his emotions from turning into anger.

Jerry's feet were intensely tapping the floor as the needle dug into his skin.

Five seconds later, she spoke.

"All done. See I told you we would have fun. I even know you enjoyed it from your happy feet," the nurse spoke in a child-like tone. "You have to admit it wasn't so bad."

"No, it was terrible," Jerry's broken laughter had subsided and it made room for his fire. He stared the lady dead in the eyes. Jerry felt his body form a smile with only his lips.

"Have a nice day," Jerry said like a jerk.

"Ok well thank you guys so much. Anything you ever need you can always come to me! Bye Jerry. Keep having fun today!" the woman said as she skipped out of the room.

"What was that about? You were terrible to her," Dominick said angrily at Jerry. "Are you kidding me?"

"I don't care. Tell that lady to read a room," Jerry yelled.

"Both of you relax," Ella stepped in. "Jerry, don't yell in here. And Dominick. How could you really get mad at him? Honestly, I would have probably behaved the same way if I was him."

Jerry panted like a dog. Dominick stayed quiet for a moment. He then spoke softly.

"Yeah. I guess you're right."

About 15 minutes later another voice emerged from behind the curtains.

"Can I come in?"

"Yes," Dominick responded.

"We are ready for you in the operating room," said a young man. "Do you want us to wheelchair you or can you walk?"

"I can walk," Jerry said normally as he tried to stand up. His body was as flexible as a brick. His bones cracked as he tried to stand up for the first time in a while.

"I got you bro," the man rushed over and put out his arms. "How you been?"

A hint of life showed in his smile.

“I’m doing alright. How about you?” Jerry responded.

“This isn’t about me. I am here for you. I’m only doing good if you are doing good,” the man said in a genuine voice. He continued with the same tone.

“Before we leave though, you have to give your parents a hug and kiss. Then we can get out of here.”

Jerry then happily gave his hugs and kisses to his parents.

“Ok now we can leave. That is my number 1 rule,” he said proudly while shaking Dominick and Ella’s hands.

Jerry followed the man out and they set out for the operating room.

“We have a little bit of a walk. Anything you want to talk about?” The man looked alongside him at Jerry.

“Not really. I am just happy to get out of that room. I only saw two ladies today and they both were getting on my nerves,” Jerry replied.

The man let out a chuckle.

“You think I don’t know that. Try working with them.”

Jerry’s face had found its color. He hoped this walk would last a long time.

"Can I be honest with you? I am very tired. I stayed up too late last night playing Minecraft," the man said.

"Are you kidding me? Stop it," Jerry answered.

The man froze for a second as he felt a switch in the conversation.

"I love Minecraft. That is my favorite game of all time," Jerry exclaimed.

The man's expressions returned stronger than before as he spoke.

"You know I would beat you so bad right?" he said as he used his ID to open up two massive double doors.

"You wish," Jerry jokingly went back at him. His walking speed increased.

After a brief minute, the two guys were met with a massive white room. There was a table lying in the middle. A massive crane reached out over the top of this table like it was an arcade machine. Everything seemed to be scrubbed clean to perfection.

There were many people scattered around this room. Everyone came up to Jerry and introduced themselves. Although Jerry couldn't remember even one name through the Taylor Swift song blasting in the background, he stood taller.

“Yo, you kidding me Kaitlyn?” the man screamed past the huge pieces of equipment in this room. Jerry saw the word *CAUTION* written in red on every device.

“I’m so sorry. I’m so sorry,” said a young female in a white coat standing in a corner on her phone. She started running towards Jerry.

“I’m Kaitlyn. It is nice to meet you. I hope my friend here is not annoying you too much. He does that a lot.”

“Get outta here,” the man said while giving her a little nudge.

“What’s your favorite song?” Kaitlyn asked. “Let me put it on the speaker.”

“Good idea,” said the man. “I guess you do have a brain up there.”

She made a mocking face towards him. Then they both turned to Jerry.

Jerry couldn't help but form a smile only with his teeth.

"I'm good, thank you guys though. This is just right."

Tool Acquired: Awareness

APPLYING THE TOOL

Jerry walked quicker to the operating room because of a Minecraft comment.

People walk faster for you when relationships become personal, not transactional.

There's a Minecraft comment in every room.

Find it.

On just another ordinary day, Jerry had to miss being in school with his friends. Instead, he found himself in the thick air of the waiting room wearing a Pirates shirt.

Just another D-Day. Just think you're fine and it will be fine. Pressure is on the doctors, not me. Just relax.

Jerry constantly kept reminding himself of these concepts. However, he felt his words just bouncing right off the walls of his head. He kept trying over and over again, but nothing happened—or so he thought.

"Hey Jerry. It's me again," Kiara said with a smile. "Follow me. Your room is ready for you."

She spoke as if she worked at a hotel. The only difference was, Jerry didn't reserve this room by choice.

The family walked to their room and Dominick's eye barely caught something.

As everyone was about to enter Jerry's small cubicle, Dominick stopped.

Dominick had seen an open room with many people sitting on chairs. The people were divided into groups. One person per group had a tube connected to a tall device on wheels.

"Why are there people outside?" Dominick asked Kiara.

"Well, you guys are actually very lucky today. As you know, chemotherapy dates aren't very flexible. And we have too many kids that need it today. We don't have enough rooms, so some people unfortunately have to be outside."

Everyone stepped inside the cubicle and Kiara continued.

"You guys were lucky enough to have been scheduled on the paper early."

"Oh my god," Dominick responded. "That really sucks. Imagine doing this without privacy. We are extremely lucky."

There was a tall device on wheels inside of the room.

Jerry gulped as he turned towards his whiteboard. Although he could never understand any of the words on the board, he didn't even recognize one.

"Rituximab," Ella called out in confusion. This was the same word that Jerry was looking at strangely.

"Yes. It is a very new chemotherapy, but the team agreed to try it on Jerry today. It is supposed to target the bad cells, but not the good ones. It takes a long time, so we put it at the end."

"Oh man," Jerry couldn't help himself. "Did you say try it on me?"

"Well, I am sorry. This medicine has been tried extensively before we are giving it to you. You will be okay."

Kiara took a second and then continued.

"It can take a long time because it is incredibly strong. If we give you too much, you may have a reaction. So, we must give it incredibly slowly."

"So, we are going to be here for a while it seems like," Dominick threw in the conversation.

"My shift lasts until 8 p.m. today. That would be twelve hours. If everything runs smoothly, you shouldn't be here past my shift. So let's just hope for that," Kiara responded.

Jerry kept forcing a thought into his brain:

If you think you're fine, then you're fine.

"Let's get the first IV in you to get us started," Kiara said to Jerry who was deep in thought.

"I recommend you go get a second nurse to help you here," Dominick said with a chuckle. "You are going to earn your money today."

Kiara smiled at Dominick. The light-hearted tone of this joke helped pull away from the word RITUXIMAB written on the board.

Kiara left the room and came back with another nurse.

This lady was incredibly short with dyed red hair. She wore glasses that were bigger than her face.

"I got the best here for you," Kiara pointed at the woman she brought in.

The woman's vibrant hair was no match for her personality.

"Oh, stop it," the woman replied as she looked at Jerry. "Don't worry about a thing, chicken wing. We got your back, especially because Kiara is the best."

Is there something with nurses calling each other the best? It's a little weird now. Jerry thought and chuckled.

Kiara tried to open her mouth but was cut off by the woman.

"Don't talk. You're the best. Now let's do this, we're wasting time."

They started laughing as they set-up the scene.

"Wait," Kiara exclaimed. "We are forgetting something."

"So, we have three chemotherapies for Jerry today," Kiara looked at Jerry's parents. "Technically, we don't need to do two IVs today. We could do all three chemotherapies separately. You guys have the option of doing one at a time through one IV."

Kiara took a breath and continued.

"The trade-off is that it would take a much longer time. It is your call, but the two IVs could save a lot of time."

"We'll take the two IVs," Dominick immediately said.

"Woah. Woah. Woah. That's because you're not getting them," Jerry yelled out.

Jerry turned to the nurses and spoke in a normal, charming voice.

"We'll take the one IV."

"We are going to be here until tomorrow," Dominick rebutted.

"For you to go sit on the couch. Dad, I know you have nothing to do tonight," Jerry wasn't going down without a fight.

The two nurses might as well have just started eating popcorn. They acted like they were watching a drama movie at the cinema.

"It doesn't mean that we need to be here until tomorrow. We have work in the morning," Dominick responded strongly.

Luckily, Kiara got out of her leather recliner and chimed in.

"Honestly, I would go with the two IVs. The rituximab takes a long time. Let's get to it as quickly as we can."

"Yeah, you heard the lady," Dominick said to Jerry and then turned to the nurses. "Two IVs please."

Both nurses put their heads down. They were ready to go almost instantly.

For a moment, Jerry's mind totally forgot about his fear of needles. It was cluttered with one weirdly spelled word: rituximab.

The two ladies had cleaned his arm and were now ready to stick him.

"Don't tell me when," Jerry's mind totally reminded his fear of needles.

His breathing intensified as his toes repeatedly bounced off the floor. His shirt had wet indents from his teeth biting.

After what felt like an eternity, Kiara spoke.

"All done. You were amazing."

The other lady immediately followed her up.

"Can I get you a warm blanket for how amazing you were?"

"If I just did amazing, then I don't even want to imagine what bad looks like," Jerry laughed as he felt the positive vibes in the room. "No, thank you. I'm good."

"No, I am sorry but I want to get you one. They feel so good, you don't understand," the red-haired nurse exclaimed as she ran out of the room.

"She's crazy but I do agree with her," Kiara said as she hooked Jerry up to the machine.

The lady came barging into the room. She came to a complete halt and gently placed the blanket on Jerry.

"Wow. Okay. I can't lie, that is awesome. But please take it off. I am going to be baking in a minute," Jerry beamed as he removed the blanket.

"Yeah, fair enough. I will put it in the corner," said the nurse.

"Hey. Look what I have to work with," Kiara turned to Dominick and Ella with a smirk. "I'm working over here and she is just trying to overheat your son."

The red-haired nurse started bursting out laughing, while Kiara kept a strong face.

"I knew that would work," Kiara said. "I go there off of you Jerry. You are welcome."

Kiara waited for her coworker to take a breath and she continued.

"You are all hooked up. You have the two chemotherapies going. You know the drill. Need anything just hit the button. Go on your phone. Order food from the menu. Don't ask this crazy for a blanket. And you are all set."

"Okay. I'll be normal and just leave," the red-haired nurse slouched her head and shoulders noticeably. She took a step for the door.

As she stood in the doorway, she spoke at lightning speed and then ran away.

"If you need a hot blanket let me know."

Jerry looked at his parents to share a laugh.

"I love her, but she is crazy. She even knows it. Really good nurse though," Kiara gave her honest evaluation.

"Ok, but seriously. If you need me hit the button. See you guys later."

Kiara had left the room and Ella spoke.

"Now we have a blanket for if you get cold."

"You are only cold if you think you are cold," Jerry instantly remarked.

"So if you think your arm isn't hooked up to that slowly dripping bag, does it mean it's not?" Dominick rebutted.

"Ha. Ha," Dominick jokingly said as he lay back in his chair. "You're never too smart for your old man."

Unbeknownst to Dominick, this concept had been running through Jerry's head all day.

"No, it doesn't because that is physical. It's a fact. The word 'cold' isn't a fact. It's subjective. If you think it is cold, doesn't mean I do," Jerry said with a smirk.

"Ha. Ha. Ha. Ha," Jerry said mockingly. "He who laughs last, laughs loudest."

Jerry gave him a tough guy look and continued. He won this argument and had to ensure his father knew.

"How you like them apples? How does it feel?"

"Whatever man. Just go on your phone already."

For the next several hours Jerry felt as if he was lying on his living room couch. He passed the time by playing videogames on his phone.

Jerry switched from game to game as he got bored quickly. Before he knew it, Kiara came through the curtain.

Kiara inspected the clear bags. Each one had a toxic symbol on it that was completely flat.

"Ok we are making real progress here. We can move onto the rituximab," Kiara said in a friendly tone.

Kiara removed the two bags and put another in its spot. They all looked identical to Jerry—just a paper bag with a toxic symbol.

"How are you Jerry?" Kiara asked. "I am about to get this started. There shouldn't be a problem, but I will stay with you for a couple minutes."

"Beep," the machine sounded.

Kiara stayed very quiet for a solid minute. She never looked away from the screen.

"It's going," Kiara turned towards Dominick and Ella. "It is just extremely slow. At this pace you will be here way past my shift. I will try to speed it up as much as I can."

"Whatever you say. We trust you," Dominick responded.

Kiara's face became glued to the screen again. After a couple of sounds, the machine sounded again.

"Beep."

Kiara monitored Jerry as his body started to shake.

Within seconds, Jerry had lost control of his body. He was violently bouncing on the bed. He felt the muscles move uncontrollably around his bones.

Kiara immediately turned to the machine and started hitting many buttons. Then, she pulled out a mini device from her pocket and hit a red button.

While Kiara was flipping out, Dominick naively spoke.

"Hey Ella, grab him the blanket from the corner. He's cold. He's shaking."

This is only bad if you think it is bad. Jerry thought as he shut his eyes.

"I am not cold Dad," Jerry said with minor annoyance in his voice.

"Yes you are. You are shaking, get him the blanket," Dominick responded.

"Dad, I am not cold. The blanket is useless," Jerry answered very rationally.

As soon as those words left Jerry's mouth, countless nurses flooded the room. They talked incredibly fast and pulled out a tablet from the cabinet. This tablet was an emergency line for medicine at the pharmacy.

Although Jerry's body was forcefully shaking out of his control, his mind stayed still. He had full control.

"Did you order it? Did you order it?" one lady said to another as she dropped the tablet.

"Yes, take a look. I think it's the right one," The nurse presented it to the crowd.

"Ok good. That is right," one lady responded.

As everyone was collaborating, a lady with dyed red hair came out of nowhere and sprinted through the cloud. She held a syringe as she ran for Jerry's IV line.

Without talking to anyone, she immediately inserted the syringe in the line and pushed.

As if it was magic, Jerry's body stopped viciously moving away from him. The bed's earthquake had quickly subsided.

When Jerry reopened his eyes, he saw the red hair fall over him. Her hand was on his arm.

"You alright there?" she asked. "I told you I had your back."

"Thank you," Jerry mumbled. "Thank you very much."

Every other nurse in the room quickly ran out as soon as they could. They probably had their own patients to be attending to.

Kiara clapped with a huge smile on her face.

"I told you she was a good nurse."

"Oh please," the lady with the red hair responded. "Just had to make sure he was okay."

"You were like a hero. We thank you very much," Dominick said to the lady with his heart.

"Don't worry about me. It's just my job. I would love to stay but I have to get back to my room. I'll see you Kiara. Call me if you need," The lady waved goodbye to Jerry as she left.

"I told you she's a good nurse," Kiara said, shaking her head as she returned to the machine. She spoke.

"Well, now we have to go slower. I'm sorry but this is going to take a lot longer now. This bag will be empty at 2 a.m."

"Nope, don't worry about time at all. We will stay here as long as we need," Dominick quickly answered.

Kiara had left the room after she set up the machine. An older lady had walked in as Kiara walked out.

The room that was just flooded with energetic millennials had been replaced by a single old lady.

"Hello everyone. I am the assisting hospital manager tonight," She sat on the window sill next to Jerry. "Are you okay?"

"Yeah, I am okay. I was annoyed with this guy," Jerry pointed to his father. "He kept telling me the reason I was shaking was because I was cold. I told you I wasn't cold."

The older woman chuckled.

"Yeah, I was wrong," Dominick said softly.

"I know you were. But you were insistent on the stupid blanket. It would have been useless," Jerry replied, slightly annoyed.

"Ok I admit I was wrong. But how did you know what was going on? I mean how did you even think straight? Your body was jumping," Dominick questioned.

"I just used my brain. It was pretty obvious," Jerry said with confusion.

"Ok, I don't think so. But even if it was obvious, how did you stay together? That was a crazy scene," Dominick continued his question.

Jerry immediately smiled.

"It's only crazy if you think it is crazy. Besides, why would I go act up? What does that do? It only adds more craziness in this room."

The lady raised herself off the window sill.

"I'm leaving this room. He doesn't need me."

Tool Acquired: Composure

APPLYING THE TOOL

The shaking of the body wasn't important. The stillness of the mind was.

This feeling is internal; it cannot be activated from physical objects, only you can.

The blanket couldn't provide control of the mind.

Never reach for your blanket.

It was 8:30 a.m. and Jerry found himself in a familiar room lying on a bed. His arm was connected to a machine through two different IVs.

Jerry was very skeptical of the tubing in his arm. He never moved it, rather he covered it up with a paper towel.

“Bro,” Jerry exclaimed. “I am actually so annoyed.”

Jerry put his phone down and threw his head back.

“I can't win a game to save my life. I can't with just my right hand,” Jerry took a quick breath. “And I keep getting school notifications blocking my screen every five seconds. They just love to load me up with assignments.”

Dominick replied with confusion.

“Ok, so what’s the problem? That’s what school does.”

“Yeah but like it’s just so much. By the time we get home I can’t do it all,” Jerry responded emotionally.

“I’m sure you can do some of it now?” Dominick replied in a rational tone.

“Dad, I don’t know if you know this, but I have one hand! Look at my other one!” Jerry said in a loud voice.

"You can play your videogames though," Dominick remarked.

Jerry looked down. His emotion had subsided by the strength of this comment. Left with no other option, Jerry tried one last-ditch effort.

"Ok yeah, but I don't want to."

Dominick fired back in a second.

"Well then don't complain that everything builds up on you. Don't complain if you are behind. I won't feel bad for you at all. Not a bit."

"But Dad," Jerry spoke in a soft tone. "Do you see where I am?"

"And what?" Dominick quickly answered.

The room became uncomfortably still.

"Look Jerry. This stinks. I am not going to lie to you, it is extremely unfortunate. But life doesn't stop coming at you. You can't either."

Jerry stared at him with confusion for a couple of seconds. He then said one word.

"What?"

Dominick was eager to continue.

"Nobody cares about what you are going through. You still need to work to put those "As" on the transcript. You still need to pay bills. You still need to do everything."

Dominick took a deep breath and laid the wood.

"If anything, you are being incredibly lazy. You are on a bed with nothing but time and you are just throwing it. I don't care that you have one arm. Leverage what you do have. You have a hand, internet, and a lot of time. Do something."

Jerry stared blankly at the ceiling. This time it wasn't out of confusion. He felt a pain way harsher than the chemicals in his arms.

Jerry had felt the pain of himself. Not only was he wasting time, he was trying to justify it.

Jerry looked over his shoulder. He saw massive pieces of equipment with more tubes than a spaghetti dinner. He looked down and saw his arm was connected to it.

The cancer isn't in my body. It's in my mind. That's really why I am here.

"You know what Dad? You are right. You couldn't be more right," Jerry talked in an honest voice.

His father just shrugged his shoulders. He had one final line.

"If there is a will, there's a way."

That was it. Jerry had found his line.

"Yep, that's enough. I'm doing my history assignment right now."

Jerry worked on this quick history assignment. It probably took the average student a half hour. Jerry spent over an hour on it. However, he didn't care if it took two days. He was giving his mind chemotherapy.

As Jerry went to submit his history assignment, an announcement intrigued him. Although he got the same message every 7 a.m., Jerry had never once bothered to pay it any mind.

CLICK HERE TO VIEW ITINERARY FOR ITALIAN CLASS TODAY

Jerry smirked as he couldn't stop his thumb. He had to go for it. His eyes beamed.

12:00: Quizlet Live on Italian Household Vocabulary

It was close to 10 a.m. and Jerry's thumb immediately swiped to his messages.

"Yo Chris. Please send me the Quizlet Live link when he puts it on the board. I want in."

For the next hour, Jerry attacked his teacher's online flashcard set. Although Italian household vocabulary wasn't the most useful thing in school, he never once questioned it.

After every single round, Jerry checked the number of incorrect answers. It didn't go down every single time, but he didn't care. Nothing stopped his thumb from feeding his mind.

Jerry finished one round with 100 percent accuracy. But he wasn't done yet. He didn't want to go until he got everything correct. He went until he couldn't get it wrong.

"Can I come in?" a voice came from behind the curtain.

A tall lady with dark hair and an unfamiliar mask had walked in. Jerry instantly was thrown off as her coat wasn't white; it was black.

"Don't worry everybody. I am not a doctor. I don't claim to be a doctor. I don't even want to be a doctor. I'm an actress here in New York."

The family all put their guard up.

"I know what you guys are wondering. But I am just here if you guys want some company. That's all I am. You can tell me to get lost if you want," the lady said.

Her words were kept afloat by her charisma. She pierced through the discomfort of the situation like it was butter.

Jerry's mind was stuck on Italian vocabulary and didn't know what to say. Dominick looked straight as he shook his head slowly. Ella shrugging her shoulders and looking up was the best answer the lady received.

Despite the lack of enthusiasm, the woman saw an opportunity.

"I want to stay here," she said confidently as she walked over to Jerry.

"How are you today?" The woman's authentic smile showed despite her mask. "I'm not a doctor. You can trust me."

"I'm okay, thanks for asking," Jerry responded.

"Are you busy or do you want to play a game?" asked the lady.

Jerry didn't even have to think.

"At 12, I have to join an online game with my Italian class. I am going to crush them. I'm free right now though."

"What do you mean?" the lady questioned in a genuine way.

"Well my class plays this online game called Quizlet. The teacher put the code on the board, so I texted my friend to give it to me when it comes out. I studied the words for the last hour. I am a machine."

"Now that's my boy," Dominick interjected loudly. He then spoke to the lady.

"Before I was getting frustrated with him. He was complaining about his work piling up. I told him to just do it now while he can. He was just playing video games before."

The lady turned to Jerry and shrugged.

"Your dad is right. He may think it's annoying but he's right. Want me to test you on the vocab?"

"Oh no," Jerry chuckled. "I promise you I am so ready. They don't stand a chance. I see you have some cards. Let's play with them."

"Now that is what I am talking about," Dominick interjected again. "You studied and now you can play. That's the right order."

Dominick reached for Ella for a high-five. She happily complied.

The lady reached for a pop-up table and put the cards on it. This table setup was the best one he'd seen in the hospital so far. No tubes, green caps, or cauldrons—just a true game.

Jerry lost every single game they played. However, he wasn't annoyed about losing like before. For some reason, these losses felt easier. He felt easier.

The room had completely changed. The silence was demolished by the sounds of laughter.

"Jerry, it's almost 12," Ella interrupted another card game that Jerry was losing.

"Already? I was just about to win again," Jerry said with a wide smile.

"Yeah alright tough guy," the lady responded with a smirk.

"Can you come back in a couple of minutes after I beat my class? It will be quick," Jerry asked the lady.

"Okay, I will," the lady responded. "But one thing. You better win though. If you don't, I'm leaving."

The two of them shook hands before the lady left the room.

Jerry cracked his knuckles and picked up his phone.

They're not ready. Jerry thought with an evil smirk.

At 12:05, Jerry received a message from Chris.

The code is

At 12:06, Chris followed up.

MXG-013

Jerry entered himself in the game and took a breath.

At lightning speed, Jerry's thumb raced around his phone. Every single box he hit turned green. And after a minute, confetti floated down his screen as his name bounced on top of the podium.

"I got the first round," Jerry yelled without looking away from his screen. "Two more. Two more."

"Come on! Let's go!" Jerry tossed his phone beside him. Although his arm was tied down, his spirits weren't.

"I won it all. First place all three times. I did it!" Jerry continued.

The lady rushed back into the room.

"I hear screaming. How bad did you lose?" she questioned with a smile.

"I didn't. I won all three. I told you. I told you," Jerry screamed. "Thanks for your help."

"Thank yourself," she replied as her smile grew.

"Ring, Ring."

"Wait, I got one more message from my friend," Jerry said as he opened it.

He read the text message out loud.

At 12:13: *The class wasn't happy.*

"But I am," Jerry yelled uncontrollably. His volume became too loud as he continued.

"I won!"

"Jerry," Dominick screamed to match Jerry's tone.

"You won here, but don't get it confused. You didn't win by beating your class. You won by overcoming something more important. Yourself."

Tool Acquired: Resilience

APPLYING THE TOOL

Jerry was fighting a disease on a hospital bed. But that wasn't the biggest battle.

The true cancer was the lack of control of his mind.

Beating his classmates meant nothing. The real win was giving his mind chemotherapy.

Important Message

"Cancer, I Thank You" was written by a 17-year-old with no literary experience, not even in Honors English. No professional help was involved either. However, he felt a fire to tell his story with the purpose of inspiring and connecting. That fire is way more powerful than status, background, or money can ever be.

In YOUR pursuit of dreams, an ongoing fire coupled with the application of these tools can push you way past anyone with just talent.

Key word there: application. Reading this book isn't enough. Knowing all the information in the world is useless if you choose to do nothing with it. You must embrace these concepts in order to reap the benefits.

I capitalized the word YOUR because this is totally your journey. You must first identify where you are lacking. Then, you must find it within yourself to change. That is an incredibly hard challenge, but a better version of you is waiting on the other side.

People may help you during your process, but nobody can find it for you. I hope these tools in the book can help you uncover it, but it must be something that you pull from inside yourself. It may be covered with the past, hatred, and many other things. But I have good news:

It is there!

Once you grab onto it, never lose it. Never allow anyone to take it from you. It is yours and only you have control over it.

And just remember:

Nobody knows your destiny.

To that Kid,

In case you are wondering. The answer is yes. I am Jerry.

I did everything here for you. I pulled my darkest experiences out of me for you. I don't want you to make the mistakes I made. Save yourself the pain and learn from mine.

I hope this book proves a couple of things to you:

You *are* heard. I hear you.

You *are* seen. I see you.

You *are* understood. I get you.

I am always in your corner. I just gave you the information I wish I could tell 14-year-old Anthony sitting on the dryer.

Now go live your life to the fullest extent. If you ever feel lost on your journey, this blueprint is always yours.

I still only ask one thing: Please help the *next kid*.

Love,

Anthony Onnembo

As I stated in my Mission Statement, I aimed to help people overcome their adversity and experience what life has to offer. I would love to hear the impact that embracing these tools has made in your life.

Email: aonnembo15@icloud.com

Instagram: @the_real_ao__

www.ingramcontent.com/pod-product-compliance
Lightning Source LLC
LaVergne TN
LVHW020717110826
845149LV00012B/2308

* 9 7 9 8 9 9 5 5 5 8 6 0 6 *